IMAGES of America

CLEVELAND COUNTY IN WORLD WAR II

Foreword

Our book begins with an apology: we could not include each person in Cleveland County who was in service or who contributed on the home front. Consider these facts: about 6,500 people from Cleveland County served during World War II. About 52,000 people remained in the county. Each was essential to the war effort. The fact that we did not include each person is not to diminish personal sacrifice and contribution; it was simply impossible to recognize everyone. We begin, therefore, with regret that everyone is not incorporated.

Each veteran and each supporter of the county during World War II has his or her own memories. Stanley B. Mathes, a comrade of Britton Hayes—who appears later in this volume—wrote the poem "Company D" and shared it with Britton. Douglas Hayes, Britton's son, has permitted us the use of the poem to help us understand better the sacrifices of Company D, 323rd Infantry, 81st Division. Many of Mathes's thoughts are unique to the situation of his company; some of his views and experiences, however, will ring true for other veterans and their families and may stir other past memories for those who gave their best also.

This is D Company speaking.
The company of mortar and gun.
We have been through hell together
And then had a lot of fun.

We began our training at Rucker.
They drilled us night and day.
Then we maneuvered in Tennessee,
Sweating it all the way.

We traveled next to Arizona.
On the desert we sweated some more.
San Luis Obispo was our next stop,
Making beachheads on California's shore.

We boarded a ship for overseas.
In convoy we crossed the blue,
Had jungle training and more landings
On the island of Oahu.

We fought on the coral of Peleliu
In the mountains and on the shore.
Then after a rest in New Caledonia,
We asked them to send us some more.

They sent us next to Leyte
Where we trained to invade Japan,
But they quit while we were training.
They just turned tail and ran.

Now we are going to Aomori
To occupy their home.
Then back to the USA again,
Never more to roam.

This is D Company speaking.
Our comrades have not died in vain.
It will ever be our job to see
That war never rages again.

(On the front cover) A United States Marine bugler, 4th Marine Division, sounds taps for comrades who fell in the invasion of Roi Island in the Kwajalein Atoll, one of the first of the Japanese territories to fall. This February 1944 photograph is courtesy of Ernest A. Cummins, Alice Inez Cummins, and the Office of the Chaplain, Second Army, Baltimore, Maryland.

IMAGES
of America

Cleveland County in World War II

Anita Price Davis and James M. Walker

ARCADIA
PUBLISHING

ISBN 978-0-7385-1772-8

Published by Arcadia Publishing
Charleston, South Carolina

Printed in the United States of America

Library of Congress Control Number: 2004116667

For all general information, please contact Arcadia Publishing:
Telephone 843-853-2070
Fax 843-853-0044
E-mail sales@arcadiapublishing.com
For customer service and orders:
Toll-Free 1-888-313-2665

Visit us on the Internet at www.arcadiapublishing.com

Background

The decade of the 1930s brought economic hardship to the nation and to the world. War had already begun abroad and was beginning to spread from nation to nation like an uncontrolled forest fire. On Sunday, December 7, 1941, the flames of the Japanese attack on Pearl Harbor seared the United States. The following day, President Roosevelt predicted that December 7 "would live in infamy." After his speech, the United States Congress declared war against Japan; World War II had begun.

World War II hit Cleveland County, North Carolina, particularly hard. The population of the county at that time was approximately 58,055. More than 6,500 Cleveland residents—11% of the total population of the county—took part in the war. The state of North Carolina had 361,000 people who served in the military. Because there were 100 counties in the state, the county sacrificially gave nearly twice its share. Cleveland County lost 190 fine young men. Cleveland County ranked 9th in the number of service personnel in World War II. Only eight North Carolina counties surpassed Cleveland in the number in the military: Mecklenberg, 20,836; Guilford, 19,192; Forsyth, 14,266; Buncombe, 13,156; Wake, 12,068; Gaston, 11,605; Durham, 9,033; Alamance, 7,176. Even when Germany surrendered on May 8 and when Japan capitulated on August 14, 1945, Cleveland County military personnel completed their tours of duty and endured continued exposure to illness and to danger.

Blue stars hung in windows to mark loved ones in service. Blue stars changed to gold as telegrams and letters arrived to announce losses. With 11% of the county's population on active duty, almost every home felt the effects of the war. Cleveland County women and retirees went to work to replace those at war. County textile plants produced war goods, operated on full schedule, and called for many additional workers. Cleveland County citizens "had to shoulder the additional load and double production, in mills, on farms, with two men instead of eight. But long hours of production were not the entire story. Many of these workers were connected with the various branches of the Office of Civilian Defense, which took up what little leisure time they had." (Clarence Griffin, *History of Rutherford County, 1937–1951*, 1952, pp. 18-19)

Contents

ACKNOWLEDGMENTS

Real Heroes: Rutherford County Men Who Made the Supreme Sacrifice in World War II, by Anita Price Davis with James M. Walker, began a series of volumes telling of the sacrifices and services of local veterans and their families. *Real Heroes* told of the 140+ Rutherford County men who lost their lives during World War II. Soon after the publication of *Real Heroes*, Rutherford County residents began to ask, "What about those of us who came home? Where is our book?" or "What about those of us who served on the home front? May we have our stories told?" *Rutherford County in World War II* began preserving the accounts of Rutherford County men and women who served their nation during the 1940s. After the publication of *Rutherford County in World War II* and *Real Heroes*, phone calls and inquiries began to pour in from other veterans, their families, and friends who were not a part of either previous volume. Jim and Anita soon realized that one book was not enough to record the contributions of Rutherford County residents who performed their duties. The series continued with *Rutherford County in World War II, Volume II*. The series, however, was not complete.

The Price family resided in Cleveland County for many years and owned stores in the county for more than half a century. Anita's mother worked in the Cleveland County store while her husband was in service, and Anita's grandfather P.R. Price carried Anita on his hip throughout the day at the Cleveland County store. In the 1960s, Anita worked at the *Shelby Star* for a summer before she began four years of teaching at Morgan School in Shelby; this newspaper work, her many years of church membership in Cleveland County, and her close association with the school children and their parents renewed her acquaintance with the county and its citizens. Anita felt a particular bond with the people of Cleveland County. As a professional photographer in Cleveland County and an employee of SportPix, Inc., James M. Walker had also developed a fondness for the area and a respect for the county residents. Jim and Anita decided to continue the story of those who gave by featuring Cleveland County.

We have many people to thank. The Cleveland County Senior Center, the Broad River Genealogical Society, and Boiling Springs Baptist Church allowed us to interview veterans. Our friend Louise Hunt scanned photographs so we could return valuable documents and treasured mementos immediately. Dedicated friends Annette Martin, Dan Martin, and Ned Cash (U.S.A.F., retired) gave time and expertise. Douglas Hayes and Billy Seay continue to give tirelessly and unselfishly. Interested individuals encouraged veterans, their families, and their friends to contact us. *The Shelby Shopper*, *The Shelby Star*, local radio stations, and area churches announced interview days. We are grateful to all these people and organizations, and especially to the veterans and their families and friends. The result of these united efforts is *Cleveland County in World War II*. The story is begun!

In honor of Cleveland County veterans,

their families, and those who served on the home front

In memory of those who sacrificed their lives

INTRODUCTION

In the late 1930s, Europe was falling under the influence of Nazism, Fascism, and Communism. The Japanese Empire, characterized by its totalitarian form of government, was striving for hegemony over East Asia. Ripples of this turmoil were spreading throughout the world.

In the pre-war years, Chancellor Adolf Hitler was rapidly re-arming the German military as he planned his world conquest. The photo above shows Hitler's troops "goose stepping" as they parade their colors. (From the collection of William "Bill" Walker.)

Price's Store was a landmark at the Cleveland–Rutherford County line. P.R. ("Pop") Price established this general store in the 1930s. The establishment became one of the first "shopping centers" in the area. Price intended to sell everything at one stop, and his family members operated the other establishments. The stores served for the exchange of news over the pickle barrel and around the pot-bellied stove. This 1939 photograph shows P.R. proudly leaning on the gas tank. (From the co-author's personal collection.)

P.R. Price's home was across Highway 74 from his store. This photograph shows the Price family, neighbors, and friends before World War II. In the second and third chairs from the right on the second row are Mr. and Mrs. P.R. Price. Seventh from right is Edward R. Price, an engineer on the Seaboard Air Line Railway during the war. Fourth from right in back is Arthur F. Price, father of Anita Price Davis; Arthur died in service on December 28, 1944. In the third row, fourth from right, is Falls W. Price, Arthur's brother, who also served. On the front row at left is Roy Donald Price, twice wounded in World War II. (Courtesy of Carolyn Grindstaff Barbee.)

One

Pearl Harbor (1941)
War Comes to Cleveland County

On December 7, 1941, 353 Japanese naval aircraft from six carriers attacked the American fleet at Pearl Harbor and the nearby U.S. Army and Navy bases. Servicemen and civilians alike were staggered and stunned by the surprise assault, which came without a formal declaration of war.

The Japanese attack sank or severely damaged 21 ships of the U.S. Pacific Fleet. American aircraft losses included 188 destroyed and 159 damaged. Even more compelling was the loss of life: 2,403 Americans died and 68 civilians were killed. Military and civilian wounded mounted to 1,178. Pictured above is the battleship *Arizona*. (Courtesy of the United States Navy.)

Pvt. James G. Blackwell, Company M, 21st Infantry Regiment, served as his unit's cook. He was just reporting for duty when the Japanese attacked; he remembers how grateful he was that the Japanese missed the ammunition dumps near Fort Shafter. He served on Christmas Island for 11 months. Private Blackwell received the American Defense Service Medal with Bronze Service Star and the Asiatic Pacific Campaign Medal with Bronze Service Star. He was discharged on April 21, 1945, after serving overseas four years, four months, and seven days. (Courtesy of James G. Blackwell.)

American sailors look in shock and disbelief at the destruction caused by the Japanese attack on Ford Island. The smoke from the burning fuel hides the devastation on Battleship Row. (Courtesy of the United States Navy.)

Two

Southwest Pacific, Solomon Islands, and New Guinea (1942–1943)

Impeding the Japanese

As 1942 opened, the Imperial Japanese Fleet ranged with amazing swiftness over vast areas of the Western Pacific and Eastern Indian Oceans. In six short months, the Japanese Imperial Forces subjugated Wake Island, Hong Kong, Singapore, the Netherlands East Indies, Thailand, Burma, the Philippines, and Northern New Guinea. For half a year, the forces of Emperor Hirohito had run wild until the Japanese commanders became intoxicated with their self-described "Victory Disease," a feeling of invincibility and inevitability. The Pacific Fleet of the United States Navy, under the command of Adm. Chester Nimitz, and American Army forces, under the command of Gen. Douglas MacArthur, finally blocked further advances in the Coral Sea, at Midway Island, at Guadalcanal, and in Southern New Guinea.

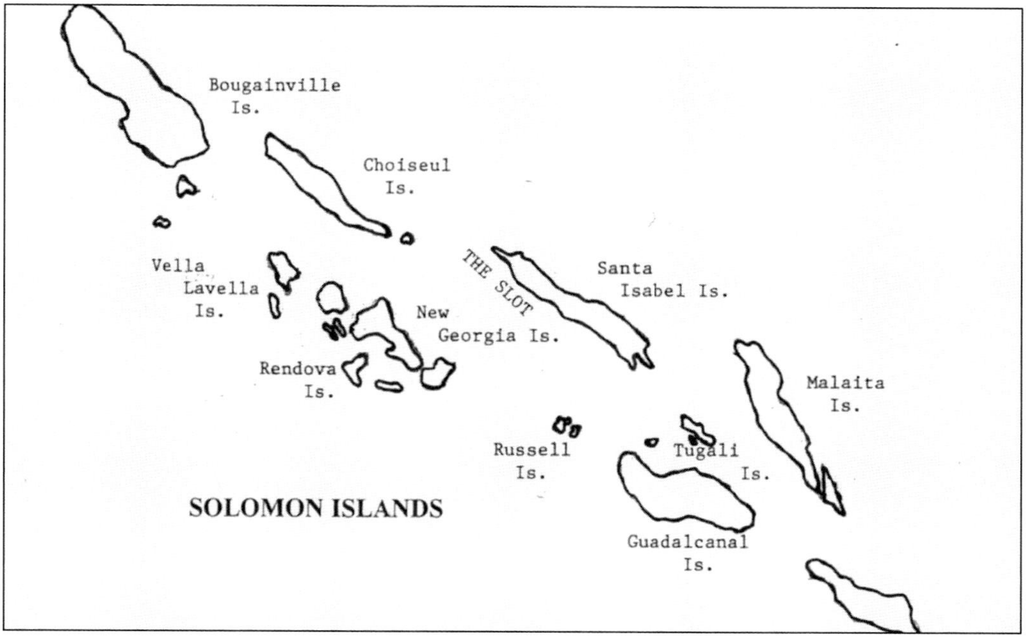

On August 7, 1942, the 1st Marine Division came ashore on Guadalcanal in the Solomon Islands. This island saw some of the bitterest fighting in the entire Pacific War. The U.S. Army later reinforced the Marines and forced the Japanese to evacuate the island in February 1943. (Sketch map courtesy of James M. Walker.)

New Caledonia, a French colony in the Southwest Pacific, supplied the 1st Marine Division on Guadalcanal. The Americal Division incorporated troops from New Caledonia; transferred to Guadalcanal, the Americal troops helped the Marines to stop and hurl back the Japanese advance. PFC Hal W. Howington, Company I, 182nd Infantry Regiment, was a light mortar crewman. For his service, he earned the American Defense Service Medal, the Asiatic Pacific Campaign Medal with two Bronze Service Stars, the Combat Infantryman's Badge, and the Good Conduct Medal. He served overseas 3 years and 28 days. (Courtesy of Hal W. Howington and family.)

Troops of the Americal Division reinforced the 1st Marine Division during operations on Guadalcanal. Here the men disembark from Higgins landing crafts. (Courtesy of the United States Army.)

In November 1943, the 3rd Marine Division invaded Bougainville near Cape Torokina. Unfortunately, PFC Joseph A. Whitesides Jr., Company M, 3rd Battalion, 21st Marines, 3rd Marine Division, did not make it ashore with his comrades. USS *McKean* sank when 57 Japanese torpedo planes from Rabaul attacked on November 17, 1943. Several mighty explosions rocked the ship before it sank. Private Whitesides's body was not recovered. His family received his Asiatic Pacific Campaign Medal, World War II Victory Medal, and the Purple Heart. (Courtesy of his great-nephew David K. Whitesides.)

In the photo above, LSTs land men, ammunition, fuel, and supplies on the beaches off Cape Torokina, Bougainville. (Courtesy of the United States Marine Corps.)

T5g. Jack E. Scruggs was a winch operator with the 604th Port Company, 387th Battalion TC. He served in the Southwest Pacific for 2 years, 9 months, and 14 days. Scruggs recalled that when he arrived in New Guinea, the natives ran because they had never seen white people. Scruggs participated in operations in Australia, the Netherlands East Indies, and New Guinea. He earned the Asiatic Pacific Campaign Medal with two Bronze Service Stars, the Good Conduct Medal, and his unit received the Presidential Unit Citation. (Courtesy of Lettie Scruggs).

In the above photograph, the Transportation Corps uses a floating crane to unload a Liberty ship at Lae, New Guinea, on April 27, 1944. (Courtesy of the United States Army.)

Three

EUROPE AND THE PACIFIC (1942–1945)

THE AIR WAR

In July 1942, the U.S. Army Air Forces began a strategic bombing campaign over occupied Europe. These raids sought to destroy the war-making capabilities of the Axis. The Allied Forces carried out their relentless bombardment by devastating and demolishing railways, factories, and troop concentrations and by interdicting communication, troop movements, and supply routes. The 8th Air Force, in cooperation with the Bomber Command of the British Royal Air Force, executed 'round-the-clock operations. The 15th Air Force, from bases in North Africa and, later, Italy, bombed southern and eastern portions of the German Reich. Helping to contain and roll back the Japanese were the 5th, 13th, 7th, and 20th Air Forces. The 5th and the 13th Air Forces operated in the Southwest Pacific, and the 7th and 20th Air Forces operated in the Central Pacific. The 14th Air Force operated in the China-Burma-India (CBI) area.

Lt. Hugh Otto "Toby" Williams was one of many young men who entered the U.S. Army Air Forces. Williams stands beside a Stearman biplane, the primary basic-training aircraft of the USAAF. Williams served as a flight instructor in 2543rd Army Air Forces Base Unit in Waco, Texas. He was a captain when discharged after serving four years and four months. (Courtesy of Jan Williams.)

S.Sgt. Emmett Graham Blanton served with the 510th Fighter Squadron as an aircraft and engine mechanic. Blanton's unit operated P-47 Thunderbolts from bases in England and, later, France and Germany; the planes harassed German troops, armored formations, convoys, and other targets of opportunity. For his services, Blanton earned the European-African-Middle Eastern (EAME) Campaign Medal with six Bronze Service Stars, the Distinguished Unit Badge, and the Good Conduct Medal. (Courtesy of the family of Emmett Graham Blanton.)

Cpl. Samuel M. Beam served as power-turret and gunsight mechanic with the 77th Fighter Squadron at Kings Cliffe, England. He participated in the Normandy, Northern France, Ardennes, Rhineland, and Central Europe Campaigns. He earned the EAME Campaign Medal with six Bronze Service Stars, and the Good Conduct Medal. He qualified as a marksman with a .45-caliber pistol. He served also in the U.S. Navy aboard the USS *Valley Forge* during Korea. (Courtesy of Una McDonald Beam.)

S.Sgt. William Harmon Carpenter served as an aircraft mechanic with the 313th Fighter Squadron, 50th Fighter Group, in Lymington, England. Sergeant Carpenter had served in the army before the war; he re-enlisted in the air force on October 22, 1941. Carpenter participated in the Normandy, Northern France, Rhineland, and Central Europe Campaigns. His unit received the Distinguished Unit Badge with one Oak Leaf Cluster. He earned the American Defense Service Medal, the EAME with five Bronze Service Stars, and the Good Conduct Medal. (Courtesy of Mrs. William Harmon [Lucille] Carpenter.)

T.Sgt. Paul Howard Carpenter, a brother of William Harmon Carpenter, served in the United States Air Force as an air police officer with the 63rd Air Police Squadron at Tyndell Air Force Base in Florida. Technical Sergeant Carpenter earned an honorable discharge for "honest and faithful service" on November 30, 1953. Paul Howard Carpenter was from the Waco community. (Courtesy of Mrs. Paul H. Carpenter.)

S.Sgt. John Mack Jenkins Jr. served as a gunnery instructor with the 713th Bomb Squadron, 448th Bomb Group, 8th Air Force, based at Seething Air Base in England. He participated in the Air Offensive Europe, Northern France, Rhineland, Ardennes, and Central Europe Campaigns. For his service Jenkins received the EAME Campaign Medal with five Bronze Service Stars, the Air Medal with Four Oak Leaf Clusters, and the Good Conduct Medal. (Courtesy of Mrs. Nell Deane Jenkins Scruggs.)

From January 1943 until February 1946, Pvt. Horace A. White served as an aircraft welder with Air Corps Headquarters, 516th Troop Carrier Group. For his service, White earned the American Campaign Theater Ribbon, the World War II Victory Medal, and the EAME Campaign Medal. He re-enlisted the day after his February 10, 1946 discharge and served as an automotive equipment operator. (Courtesy of Ned Cash.)

John Franklin Anderson joined the U.S. Army Air Forces on December 13, 1941. He served as a corporal in armament. His stations included Denver, Colorado; Barksdale Field in Shreveport, Louisiana; Foster Field in Texas; Matagora Peninsula; Salt Lake City, Utah; Hawaii; and finally Fort Stewart in Georgia. Anderson received his honorable discharge in January 1946, after more than five years of service. (Courtesy of John Franklin Anderson and family.)

Sgt. Charles Frederick Faber of the U.S. Marine Corps served as a general clerk in the Marine Wing Service Squadron 9, 9th Marine Air Wing, Fleet Marine Force. Sergeant Faber participated in the campaigns for Treasury-Bougainville and Bismarck Archipelago, the defense of Piva Yoke Airfield, and the consolidation of the Solomon Islands. The Piva Yoke Airfield operated SBD dive-bombers and the TBF torpedo-bombers. He received his honorable discharge on September 21, 1945. (Courtesy of Joan Faber.)

Sgt. Elvis H. Hamrick entered service in March 1942. He served as an aerial engineer and a gunner on a B-25. He went overseas in July 1942, and in November 10, 1944, he went missing in action. Witnesses reported Hamrick's aircraft was last seen with smoke pouring from the cockpit at Ormoc Bay, Leyte, in the Philippines. Sergeant Hamrick, a graduate of Shelby High School, was 30 at the time of his death. He earned the Purple Heart and the Asiatic-Pacific Campaign Medal. (Courtesy of Betty [Mrs. Harold] Wright.)

Capt. John Z. McBrayer was a B-24 pilot with the 14th Air Force. Stationed in Southern China, McBrayer conducted missions against Hanoi, Haiphong, Hong Kong, Hangchow, and other Japanese-occupied cities. McBrayer flew 68 missions. On April Fool's Day 1944, the prop of the inboard engine of the plane sliced through the cockpit and severed his leg. He earned the Purple Heart, the Distinguished Flying Cross, the Air Medal with Oak Leaf Cluster, the Asiatic-Pacific Campaign Medal, the World War II Victory Medal, and the Good Conduct Medal. (Courtesy of Carol McBrayer Allen.)

Thomas E. Wright had a promising career with the Boston Red Sox interrupted by World War II. Corporal Wright served in the 339th Fighter Squadron as an aircraft armorer. The 339th operated P-38s from a base near Puerto Princesa, Palawan Island, Philippines. The P-38s flew over the South China Sea, Borneo, and the Southern Philippines. Wright received the American Campaign Medal, the Asiatic Pacific Campaign Medal with three Bronze Service Stars, the Good Conduct Medal, and the World War II Victory Medal. (Courtesy of Thomas E. Wright.)

PFC Robert "Red" E. Kale served in the Headquarters Squadron, 5th Fighter Command, as a truck driver and mechanic. The 5th Fighter Command received credit for downing 2,547 Japanese aircraft in New Guinea, the Bismarck Archipelago, Southern Philippines, and Luzon. Kale drove Charles Lindbergh from the airstrip to headquarters. Kale earned the Asiatic Pacific Campaign Medal with four Bronze Service Stars, the American Campaign Medal, the Philippines Liberation Ribbon with two Bronze Service Stars, the Good Conduct Medal, and the World War II Victory Medal. (Courtesy of Mr. and Mrs. Don Jenkins.)

PFC Robert Kale had three other brothers in the military. Pvt. Alfred G. Kale, U.S. Marines, participated in operations on Palau Islands. He suffered wounds and received the Purple Heart. (Courtesy of Mr. and Mrs. Don Jenkins.)

S.Sgt. Jack B. Kale served as a squad leader for his unit in the New Guinea and Southern Philippine Campaigns. He twice received wounds and earned the Purple Heart with Oak Leaf Cluster. (Courtesy of Mr. and Mrs. Don Jenkins.)

PFC Roy H. "Tom" Kale served in the Rhineland and Central Europe Campaigns. He was in the front lines for over 100 consecutive days. His unit was a part of the 7th Army. (Courtesy of Mr. and Mrs. Don Jenkins.)

PFC Martin C. Wilkie Jr., 12th Air Depot Group, 5th Air Force, was an aircraft supercharger repairman. He remembers spending 96 days on a Liberty ship waiting for a place to land. He spent 6 weeks in Hollandia, New Guinea; 4 weeks at Leyte Gulf, Philippine Islands; and 22 days in Manila. He earned the Asiatic Pacific Campaign Medal with two Bronze Service Stars, the Philippines Liberation Ribbon with one Bronze Service Star, the World War II Victory Medal, and the Good Conduct Medal. (Courtesy of Martin Wilkie.)

Sgt. Joseph W. Costner Jr., 1st Air Cargo Resupply Squadron, served from August 8, 1942, until February 9, 1946, and participated in the CBI and Central Europe Campaigns. He served as an automotive equipment mechanic and earned the American Theater Service Medal, the Asiatic Pacific Campaign Medal with three Bronze Service Stars, the World War II Victory Medal, and the Good Conduct Medal. (Courtesy of Joseph "Joey" Costner III.)

Pvt. David C. Turner (left) served between March 27, 1946, and May 2, 1947, as a mechanic with the 9th Reconnaissance Squadron VLR. Turner flew clandestine reconnaissance missions for Chiang Kai-Shek from a secret base on the Chinese mainland. The unarmed aircraft was essentially a "flying gas tank." David Turner's most vivid memory was seeing a river blocked with logs; upon closer inspection, he saw that it was bodies of dead Chinese that the Communists had thrown in the river. For his services, he earned the Army of Occupation-Japan and the World War II Victory Medals. (Courtesy of Broadus Turner and Douglas Hayes.)

Four

North Africa, Sicily, and Italy (1942–1945)

Fighting Back

President Franklin Delano Roosevelt and British Prime Minister Winston Spencer Churchill believed that the occupation of North Africa would be a preliminary step to an invasion of Europe. This action would be the first opportunity for the young U.S. Army to face the veteran German troops in combat. On November 8, 1942, the Allies' amphibious attacks (Operation TORCH) hit three beaches: the Atlantic coast of French Morocco and the Mediterranean coasts of Oran and Algiers in Algeria. Upon the liberation of North Africa, the Allies moved on to invade Sicily and southern Italy in 1943. The fascist regime of Benito Mussolini collapsed as a result of these actions. The Germans contested the Allied advance, and the final surrender did not occur until May 1945.

On that fateful November day, the United States Army troops, under the command of Maj. Gen. George S. Patton, waded ashore and liberated Morocco in three days. (Courtesy of United States Army.)

Cpl. Ernest Reuben Allen served with the 53rd Signal Battalion attached to II Corps. Allen participated in the Algeria–French Morocco Invasion, Tunisia, Sicily, Naples-Foggia, Rome-Arno, Northern Apennines, and the Po Valley Campaigns. Allen's united helped capture Rome on June 4, 1944, two days before the D-Day Invasion of France. Allen received the EAME Campaign Medal with Seven Bronze Service Stars, the American Defense Service Medal, and the World War II Victory Medal. (Courtesy of Ernest Reuben Allen.)

PFC Robert "Rob" William Whiteside served with the 550th Parachute Infantry Battalion. Private Whiteside spoke about participating in combat jumps in Sicily, Nice, and Bastogne. He remembered glider landings in Anzio and at Cannes. He earned the Bronze Star Medal when he and two comrades attacked a German machine-gun nest near Caserta, Italy. Whiteside tried to destroy a German Tiger tank with a bazooka; he was captured after being wounded in the face and upper body and incarcerated as a POW in Stalag XIIA and IXB at Limburg An Der Lahn Hessen-Nessau. (Courtesy of Rachel Haynes Tanner and William Junius Haynes.)

J.B. Porter was a paratrooper with the "All-American" 82nd Airborne and participated in the Anzio operations in Southern Italy. Later in the war, Porter was a participant in many of the actions of the 82nd Airborne Division and in the Battle of the Bulge at Bastogne, Belgium. Porter died on January 1, 1989. (Courtesy of Carolyn Porter Shrader.)

PFC Willie Ezell Poole enlisted at 16 by lying about his age. He turned 17 while he was in basic training. Private Poole served in Battery A, 329th Field Artillery Battalion, as a heavy truck driver. He participated in the Tunisia, the Rome-Arno, and the Naples-Foggia Campaigns. He credited his survival to the grace of God. Poole received for his services the EAME Campaign Medal with three Bronze Service Stars, the World War II Victory Medal, and the Good Conduct Medal. He died on April 18, 2004. (Courtesy of Arvelena Proctor.)

T5g. Thomas P. Lee was a half-track driver who served with the 1st Reconnaissance Troop, 1st Infantry Division, "Big Red One." He and his unit participated in the Algeria, French Morocco, Tunisia, Sicily, Normandy, Northern France, and Rhineland Campaigns. Lee suffered wounds in action in France on August 16, 1944. For his services, he received the Purple Heart Medal and the EAME Campaign Medal with six Bronze Service Stars. (Courtesy of Ned Cash.)

First Sgt. William Duke Hill served in the Headquarters Company of the 601st Tank Destroyer Battalion, 3rd Infantry Division, "Rock of the Marne," and participated in operations at Anzio and the invasion of Southern France, Operation DRAGOON. Sergeant Hill's photographs of himself in uniform often show an animal with him. Upon his discharge on October 12, 1945, he had earned the EAME Campaign Medal with Bronze Service Star, the Presidential Unit Citation, the Good Conduct Medal, and the World War II Victory Medal. (Courtesy of Mrs. Mary F. Hill.)

PFC Robert Lee Parker, Company H, 363rd Infantry, 91st Infantry Division, "Wild West," served as truck driver for his unit. He and A.C. "Tom" Parker (chapter 7) were brothers. Robert Parker participated in the Rome-Arno, North Apennines, and Po Valley Campaigns. He earned the American Theater Campaign, the EAME Campaign Medal with two Bronze Service Stars, and the Good Conduct Medal. (Courtesy of Judith Parker-Proctor.)

S.Sgt. John H. Palmer Jr., 391st Ordnance Medium Automotive Maintenance Company, served 16 months in Italy as a machine gunner and as a squad leader. He suffered wounds on August 14, 1944, in the Northern Apennines and was hospitalized for four months. He returned to active service as a postal clerk in the 7th Depot Post Office. He earned the Purple Heart, the Combat Infantryman's Badge, the American Theater Campaign Medal, the EAME Campaign Medal with two Bronze Service Stars, the World War II Victory Medal, and the Good Conduct Medal. (Courtesy of Dorothy J. Palmer.)

Sgt. Judd Lee Wilkie served in an armored infantry battalion as a jeep, half-track, and tank driver. His unit was attached to the 3rd Army. He participated in the Northern France, Rhineland, and Central Europe Campaigns. His unit was in southern Bavaria at the end of the war, in Hitler's backyard at Berchtesgaden, Germany. He received for his services the EAME Campaign Medal with three Bronze Service Stars, the World War II Victory Medal, and the Good Conduct Medal. (Courtesy of Lavonia Wilkie Radford.)

PFC James M. Singleton, Company H, 3rd Battalion, 180th Infantry Regiment, 45th Division, "Thunderbird," participated in Anzio, the capture of Rome in June 1944, Southern France, Rhineland, and Central Europe Campaigns. Singleton suffered wounds on February 19, 1943, during the Anzio Campaign and still recalls the screams of the wounded and the terrible mud that all but swallowed the vehicles. He recalls the liberation of the Dachau Concentration Camp. (Courtesy of James M. Singleton.)

For his services, PFC James M. Singleton received the Purple Heart, the Bronze Star Medal, the Combat Infantryman's Badge, the American Campaign Medal, the EAME Campaign Medal with Service Stars and two Bronze Arrowheads, the World War II Victory Medal, the Army of Occupation (Germany), the Good Conduct Medal, and the French Croix de Guerre; the unit received the Presidential Unit Citation. (Courtesy of James M. Singleton.)

The 20th Combat Engineer Battalion was one of the first combat engineer units to participate in North Africa. Cleveland County resident Willard Davis of Company D wrote from North Africa to his adoptive parents, Mr. and Mrs. John Lee Davis in Mooresboro, with a special request: "Please send me a pone of cornbread." His mother obliged and mailed one to him. Here Willard is shown posing in front of his barracks during basic training. (Courtesy of Mike Davis and the family of Jessie Willard Davis.)

Standing on the beach at Gela, Sicily, Lt. Gen. George S. Patton Jr. surveys his 7th Army troops. General Patton was one of the most colorful officers in the American Army. (Courtesy of the United States Army.)

Five

CBI, Clearing the Islands, and MacArthur's Return (1943–1944)

The War Continues

By 1943, the Allies had stopped the Japanese forces and were beginning to roll them back. The U.S. Navy and the U.S. Marine Corps were advancing across the Central Pacific. The U.S. Army, with the Australian and New Zealand Forces, advanced upon the Philippines from the southwest. Allied forces in the CBI Theater were holding the line in Burma. Adm. Chester Nimitz, commander-in-chief of the Pacific Fleet; Gen. Douglas MacArthur, commander of the Southwest Pacific Area; and Lt. Gen. Joseph W. Stilwell, commander, U.S. forces in the CBI, directed the three-pronged offensive.

Gen. Douglas MacArthur is shown here shortly before wading ashore at Leyte Island, October 20, 1944. (Courtesy of the United States Army.)

S.Sgt. Robert Hal Fite Sr. served as an air traffic controller with the 140th Air Control Squadron, 5th Air Force. Sergeant Fite's stations included Milne Bay, Finschhafen, and Saidor, all in New Guinea. Sergeant Fite recalls the hot, humid climate and the excessive rainfall. The 5th Air Force used B-17s, B-25s, and A-20s; P-47s and P-51s escorted the bombers on their missions. Sergeant Fite earned the American Theater Service Medal, the Asiatic-Pacific Campaign Medal with one Bronze Service Star, the Good Conduct Medal, and the World War II Victory Medal. (Courtesy of Robert Hal Fite Sr.)

PFC Murrell E. Howard served as a cannoneer with Battery A, 45th Coastal Artillery Battalion, and participated in operations in Palau Islands and the Southern Philippines; his assignments included the Aleutians and Hawaii. Howard endured an appendectomy at a field hospital—and he was awake. Howard earned the American Theater Campaign Medal, the Asiatic-Pacific Campaign Medal with two Bronze Service Stars, the Philippine Liberation Medal, the World War II Victory Medal, and the Good Conduct Medal. (Courtesy of Janet H. Cooke.)

CPO Ray B. Wesson Sr. worked as a chef before the war. He joined a naval construction battalion—the "Seabees." The Seabees were mainly older men from the construction trade. Wesson was a mess overseer for one of these construction companies. He participated in Operation CATCHPOLE, the invasion of Eniwetok Atoll, Marshall Islands. Wesson (in helmet) is the third from left on the front row. (Courtesy of Dr. Lynn E. Wesson.)

CPO Ray B. Wesson Sr. wrote home that the island was "crawling with Japanese." After American forces secured the island, Wesson's Seabee company prepared the important atoll as a forward base for naval forces. In the late 1940s, Wesson and his wife, Grace Owens Wesson, operated a coffee shop in Lawndale and Wesson's Barbecue in Shelby. He earned the American Campaign Service Medal, the Asiatic Pacific Campaign Medal with Bronze Service Star, the World War II Victory Medal, and the Good Conduct Medal. (Courtesy of Dr. Lynn E. Wesson.)

S.Sgt Britton Hayes, Company D, 323rd Infantry, 81st Division, "Wildcat," served as a squad leader during operations on Angaur Island in the Palau chain. The Japanese had heavily fortified these coral islands, which were stepping-stones to the Philippines. In September 1944, the 81st Division successfully rooted out the Japanese defenders from their caves and bunkers. This operation opened the way for General MacArthur's return to the Philippines the following month. (Courtesy of Douglas Hayes.)

S.Sgt. Britton Hayes received for his services the Bronze Star Medal, the American Campaign Medal, the Asiatic Pacific Campaign Medal with Bronze Service Star, the World War II Victory Medal, the Combat Infantryman's Badge, the Expert Infantryman's Badge, the Philippine Liberation Ribbon, and the Good Conduct Medal. He qualified as an expert with rifle and pistol. (Courtesy of Douglas Hayes.)

Hubert Eric Johnson, United States Navy, was an aircraft radioman. He participated in the liberation of Guam. After the war, Johnson served in both the navy and the air force reserves. He retired in 1986 from the naval reserves with the rank of chief petty officer. His awards included the American Campaign Service Medal, the Asiatic Pacific Campaign Medal, the World War II Victory Medal, and the Good Conduct Medal. (Courtesy of Susan Johnson Collier.)

Sgt. Claude Hudson Blanton Jr. served with Company C, 749th Railway Operating Battalion, in New Guinea, Panay, and Luzon. The company transported POWs, ammunition, and supplies. Transferred to the 13th Air Force at Clark Air Field, Philippine Islands, he served with his brother, Sgt. John Coffield Blanton, who guarded POWs. Sgt. Claude Blanton received the Asiatic-Pacific Campaign Medal, the Philippine Liberation Medal with two Bronze Service Stars, and the Cross of Military Service from the United Daughters of the Confederacy. (Courtesy of Sara Blanton Johnston.)

Sgt. John Coffield Blanton served with the 372nd Bomb Squadron HV. Sergeant Blanton served as an aerial gunner on a B-24. He was stationed at Clark Field in the Philippines. His brother, Sgt. Claude Hudson Blanton Jr., and he served together in the Philippines. For his services, he earned the American Theater Service Ribbon, the Asiatic Pacific Campaign Medal, the Philippine Liberation Service Medal, and the Good Conduct Medal. (Courtesy of Margaret Jones Blanton and Sara Blanton Johnston.)

Sgt. Ernest A. Cummins served with the Canadian Department of Munitions and Supply in Washington, D.C. He acted as a courier between this department and the Navy Department. (Courtesy of E.A. Cummins.)

By mid-1945, Sgt. Ernest A. Cummins was serving on Leyte in the Philippines. Here are Sergeant Cummins (right) and a fellow soldier at a small monument commemorating Gen. Douglas A. MacArthur's return to the Philippines in October 1944. Sergeant Cummins earned the Army of Occupation Medal (Japan) and the World War II Victory Medal. He received his discharge from Unit Headquarters, 2nd Army, in 1946. (Courtesy of Ernest A. Cummins.)

Sgt. Mont R. Bridges served as a section leader in the 81st Cavalry Reconnaissance Troop. He participated in the Western Pacific and Southern Philippines Campaigns. He earned for his services the American Theater Medal, the Asiatic Pacific Campaign Medal with two Bronze Service Stars and Bronze Arrowhead, the Philippines Liberation Medal with Bronze Service Star, the World War II Victory Medal, and the Good Conduct Medal. (Courtesy of Annie Mae Bridges.)

Cpl. William H. Gardner Jr., Company D, 127th Infantry Regiment, 32nd Infantry Division, "Red Arrow," was originally assigned to a flame-thrower unit, but he received transfer to the infantry. In 1945, he was captured; he escaped and hid in the jungle behind enemy lines for five days. On Luzon in June 1945, after 40 straight days of combat, he suffered wounds. Gardner served overseas for 1 year, 3 months, and 16 days. Here are Gardner, his wife, and child in the Double Springs community. (Courtesy of Jerry W. Gardner.)

Cpl. William H. Gardner's tour included the occupation of Japan. He remembered making friends with the houseboys who were all named "Joe" and how they desired to come to America. Gardner (right) appears in Kochi, Japan. He earned the Purple Heart Medal, the Asiatic Pacific Campaign Medal with Bronze Services Star, the Philippine Liberation Medal, the World War II Victory Medal, the Occupation of Japan Medal, the Good Conduct Medal, and the Combat Infantryman's Badge. He qualified as an expert with the .30-caliber rifle. (Courtesy of Jerry W. Gardner.)

S.Sgt. Kenneth J. Boggs, Headquarters Company, 475th Infantry Regiment, 5307th Composite Unit (Provisional), "Merrill's Marauders," reached his assignment in India after sailing 33 days. He served overseas one year, seven months, and eight days. He recalled that Burma had "hills covered with jungle and rain that exceeded 175 inches in a year." Boggs was in charge of supply mules. He recalled an air-dropped Thanksgiving dinner in 1944 and being called away before he could eat it. He remembered a Christmas cake from his sister, as well. (Courtesy of Kenneth S. Boggs.)

S.Sgt. Kenneth J. Boggs recalled about General Stilwell that "he had only wanted trained troops and volunteers" but that he was "really glad the boys were there." Staff Sergeant Boggs received the Bronze Star Medal, the American Theater Campaign Medal, the Asiatic Pacific Campaign Medal with four Bronze Service Stars, the Combat Infantryman's Badge, the World War II Victory Medal, the Good Conduct Medal, and the Presidential Unit Citation. The photograph shows General Stilwell at the Myitkyina airfield in Burma in June 1944. (Courtesy of the United States Army.)

First Lt. Dorothy H. Cabaniss, 234th General Hospital, Chabua, Assam, India, served for more than two years in a 1,000-bed hospital located in the middle of a working tea plantation. The busiest time at the hospital was during the Battle for Burma, when American, British, Chinese, Indian, and Burmese soldiers entered the hospital. Her military specialty was general-duty nurse. Her letters described pythons, cobras, and a Thanksgiving meal with bed sheets as tablecloths and a canned turkey. She earned the Asiatic Pacific Campaign Medal. (Courtesy of Sandra Elliott.)

T4g. Martin Gold Jones, 2885th Engineer Floating Power Plant, was a surgical technician. He was the only medical man in his detachment and did everything from treating colds to performing minor surgery at his Philippine base. He was also a steamfitter during his service from March 1942 until December 1945. (Courtesy of Mrs. Martin Gold Jones, Billy Seay, and Douglas Hayes.)

Sgt. Braxton C. Scruggs, Company B, 640th Tank Destroyer Battalion, was a duty NCO who participated in the Southern Philippines and Luzon Campaigns. He earned the Asiatic Pacific Campaign Medal with one Bronze Service Star, the Philippine Liberation Service Medal with one Bronze Service Star, the World War II Victory Medal, and the Good Conduct Medal. (Courtesy of the family of Braxton C. Scruggs.)

T5g. Paul C. Wilson, 3119th Signal Service Battalion, served as an automobile mechanic in Luzon, Philippine Islands, in June and August 1945. Afterward, his unit participated in the occupation of Japan. For his services, Technician Wilson earned the Asiatic Pacific Campaign Medal, the Army of Occupation (Japan), the World War II Victory Medal, and the Good Conduct Medal. His unit earned the Philippine Presidential Unit Citation. (Courtesy of Paul C. Wilson and Ned Cash.)

To support their operations in the Pacific Theater, many specialized units existed, including port companies of the transportation corps. These units distributed all kinds of supplies. Technician Rollin Delbert Cook served as a longshoreman in the 152nd Port Company. He participated in the Southern Philippines and Luzon Campaigns and earned the Asiatic Pacific Campaign Medal with two Bronze Service Stars, the Philippine Liberation Medal, the World War II Victory Medal, and the Good Conduct Medal; he qualified as a marksman with the .30 carbine. (Courtesy Elaine C. Cosby.)

T4g. Edwin E. Harris, 342nd Harbor Craft Company, was an able seaman. He earned the American Theater Campaign Medal, the EAME Campaign Medal, the Asiatic Pacific Campaign Medal, the World War II Victory Medal, the Good Conduct Medal, and the Meritorious Unit Award. When Harris returned home to his wife Grace, their two-year-old son ran from him and hid under the bed. (Courtesy of Edwin E. Harris and family.)

Six

D-Day, the Liberation of France, and the Ardennes (1944)

European Campaigns

In the European Theater, years of training and preparation achieved culmination with the massive Normandy invasion; Gen. Dwight David Eisenhower, Supreme Allied Commander, directed this "Great Crusade." After breaking out of the beachheads, Allied forces pursued the remnants of the defeated German Army back to the borders of the Fatherland. Regrouping, the Nazis staged a last, desperate, and ultimately futile counterattack: the Ardennes Offensive.

This photograph shows members of Cannon Company, 358th Infantry Regiment, 90th Division, "Tough Hombres," who were among the troops in the Normandy Invasion. One of these soldiers (at left in back) was S.Sgt. Ralph L. Pittman. (Courtesy of Billy Seay and the family of Ralph L. Pittman.)

Coxswain William Raymon Dixon piloted a Higgins boat during the second wave of the Normandy Invasion. His wife recalls his telling of ships burning around him as he went ashore. Dixon served aboard LST-284 and LCS (L) 3. He served from February 13, 1943, until September 22, 1945, and earned the EAME with one Bronze Service Star and Bronze Arrowhead, the World War II Victory Medal, and the Good Conduct Medal. (Courtesy of Mrs. William Raymon Dixon.)

Pharmacist's Mate 3c. Jesse Lee Taylor was "volunteered" to the Medical Corps by his officer. In 1944, he served at a hospital in Southampton, England. After the invasion of France, the hospital filled with casualties, including a neighborhood boy with a shoulder wound. A short time later, the boy was back with an arm wound. The third time he came with "his dog tags around his toe." Taylor also served in the South Pacific, where he was a nurse's assistant at Noumea, New Caledonia. (Courtesy of Jeanette Ruppe Taylor.)

Pharmacist's Mate 3c. Jesse Lee Taylor received his discharge in March 1946. When Taylor had entered the service, he was 5 foot 8 inches and weighed 135 pounds; when discharged he was 6 foot 1 inch and 218 pounds. The discharging physician yelled, "Good God, Man! You found a home in the navy, didn't you?" Taylor gave a final salute and walked out the door! He earned the EAME Campaign Medal, the Asiatic Pacific Campaign Medal, and the Good Conduct Medal. (Courtesy of Jeanette Ruppe Taylor.)

PFC Hobart A. Fisher, Company B, 38th Infantry Regiment, 2nd Infantry Division, "Indian Head," served as a truck driver and an infantryman in the Normandy, Northern France, Ardennes, Rhineland, and Central Europe Campaigns. Private Fisher suffered wounds to the legs and buttocks when a mine exploded near St. Lo, France, on July 6, 1944. He rehabilitated at the 53rd General Hospital in England. Lt. Thelma Johnson of the 53rd General Hospital gave him special care. They sit together in the accompanying photograph. (Courtesy of Aaron Scott Fisher.)

After his recovery, PFC Hobart A. Fisher returned to active duty. He recalled the Lord telling him to get into a foxhole. A large shell exploded seconds later. Private Fisher's unit received the Presidential Unit Citation; he earned the Purple Heart, the Combat Infantryman's Badge, the EAME with Silver Service Star and Bronze Arrowhead, the Bronze Star Medal, the Army of Occupation Medal (Germany), the American Campaign Service Medal, the Good Conduct Medal, the Belgian Fourrageres, and the World War II Victory Medal. (Courtesy of Aaron Scott Fisher.)

PFC Dewitt Lowery, H and S Troop, 2nd Cavalry Reconnaissance Squadron, "Patton's Ghosts," served with his unit to probe the flanks of the enemy. They employed jeeps, armored cars, half tracks, and Stuart tanks to search for the weak spots in the enemy line so the American forces could exploit the German vulnerabilities. (Courtesy of Ruby S. Lowery.)

PFC Dewitt Lowery recalled how his unit went ahead of Patton's forces. Here he is armed with a M-3 submachine gun—a "grease gun." For his services he earned the EAME Campaign Medal with five Bronze Service Stars, the World War II Victory Medal, the Occupation of Germany Medal, and the Good Conduct Medal. He qualified as a marksman with the machine pistol. (Courtesy of Ruby S. Lowery.)

PFC Robert E. Sisk, Battery B, 905th Field Artillery Battalion, was brother-in-law to Dewitt Lowery. Private Sisk was a cannoneer for his unit. In September 1944, Robert recognized his brother-in-law and friend Dewitt Lowery in a passing jeep. They were able to meet in Eastern France. Sisk received the EAME Campaign Medal with four Bronze Service Stars, the World War II Victory Medal, and the Good Conduct Medal. He qualified as a sharpshooter with the carbine. (Courtesy of Ruby S. Lowery.)

PFC Blanch A. Williams was in Service Battery, 27th Field Artillery Battalion, 3rd Armored Division, "Spearhead." Williams never discussed his military service. His military discharge, however, stated that he was a half-track driver and participated in the Normandy, Ardennes, Rhineland, and Central Europe Campaigns. Private Blanch Williams earned the EAME with four Bronze Service Stars, the World War II Victory Medal, the Good Conduct Medal, and the Belgian Fourrageres. (Courtesy of Rachel L. Williams.)

T5g. Walter Dewitt Vess Sr. served as a truck driver in Battery B, 456th Coastal Artillery Battalion. Here he is in the driver's seat of a 2 1/2–ton truck with his comrades. (Courtesy of Peggy Vess.)

During 1945, T5g. Walter Dewitt Vess Sr. (right) met his brother Bill Vess (left) in Paris. During this happy reunion, they were able to sit for a photograph, which the family treasures. (Courtesy of Peggy Vess.)

T5g. Walter Dewitt Vess Sr. qualified as an expert with the Thompson .45-caliber submachine gun. Vess participated in the Normandy, Northern France, Ardennes, Rhineland, and Central Europe Campaigns. For his services, he received the EAME with five Bronze Service Stars and the Good Conduct Medal. (Courtesy of Peggy Vess.)

PFC Thomas Norris Spangler entered service on March 23, 1943. Landing in France in June 1944, Private Spangler served with Company L, 314th Infantry Regiment, 79th Infantry Division, "Lorraine." Private Spangler was killed in action on December 10, 1944, during the advance of the 7th Army on the Rhine River from the Vosges Mountains. Spangler received the Purple Heart, the Combat Infantryman's Badge, and the EAME Campaign Badge. (Courtesy of Margie Christopher.)

PFC Rafe R. Lovelace, Company A, 76th Armored Medical Battalion, 6th Armored Division, "Super Sixth," served in Normandy, Northern France, Rhineland, Ardennes, and Central Europe. In addition to his medical duties, he was the barber for the troops in his unit. Lovelace admits, "War is rough." He remembers crossing the Rhine River on a pontoon bridge in his truck. (Courtesy of Rafe R. Lovelace.)

PFC Rafe R. Lovelace (right) recalls that while driving during blackout conditions, his 2 1/2–ton kitchen truck left the road and ended upside down. Fortunately, no one received injuries. For his 3 years, 6 months, and 27 days overseas, he received the EAME Campaign Badge with five Bronze Service Stars and the Good Conduct Medal. (Courtesy of Rafe R. Lovelace.)

T5g. Jack P. Riviere, Company A, 649th Engineer Topographical Battalion, had the duty of drawing maps. After serving in the Rome-Arno Campaign, Riviere and his unit participated in Southern France, the Rhineland, and Central Europe. He earned the EAME Campaign Medal with four Bronze Service Stars and one Bronze Arrowhead, the Good Conduct Medal, and the World War II Victory Medal. (Courtesy of Catherine P. Spangler and Marjorie Riviere.)

Sgt. C.W. "Jack" Joyner served with the 1063rd Replacement Company of the 132nd Replacement Battalion. His assignment was as a supply sergeant; he issued and received quartermaster supplies. During his service in England, Jack was able to meet his brother Craig Joyner, who was also in service. (Courtesy of Mrs. Jim Lutz.)

Cpl. Hugh Q. Howington, 936th Field Artillery Battalion, was the twin brother of PFC Hal Howington. He served in the European Theatre of Operations and received the Purple Heart, the American Defense Service Medal, the Good Conduct Medal, and the EAME Campaign Badge with four Bronze Service Stars. He served overseas 1 year, 9 months, and 17 days. (Courtesy of Hugh Q. Howington.)

Sgt. Everette G. Camp served in the 1068th General Hospital in Taunton, England. The hospital moved to Rennes, France, on June 29, 1944. Six months later they moved to Nancy, France. Camp recalled boys who had lost arms, legs, and eyes. He remembered their crying and calling for their mothers. He often worked 12 to 18 hours a day, and sometimes more. He earned the EAME Campaign Medal with two Bronze Service Stars, the World War II Victory Medal, and the Good Conduct Medal. (Courtesy of Everette G. Camp.)

In November 1944, three battalions—20th Combat Engineers, 1340th Combat Engineers, and 146th Combat Engineers—of the 1173rd Engineer Group committed as infantry. Their task was to recapture Vossenack from the Germans to allow the withdrawal of the 28th Infantry Division. During this action, T5g. Jessie Willard Davis, Company D, 20th Combat Engineer Battalion, was killed. Davis was interred in the U.S. Military Cemetery in Henri Capelle, Belgium, and later moved to Sunset Memorial Cemetery in Shelby. (Courtesy of Tamy Connell, Chris Connell, and Mr. and Mrs. Max Davis.)

Sgt. Falls W. Price (above, left) trained as a medic and entered combat in France on D+17. "Bed-Check Charlie," a German bomber, harassed them each night. The German Nebelwerfer multi-barreled rocket launcher was also a threat; the "Moaning Minnies" were "frightful." Price volunteered and received assignment to Company C, 423rd Infantry Regiment, 106th Infantry Division, "Golden Lion." Sergeant Price ended the war on the French Coast near Saint-Nazaire and participated in the occupation of the German submarine pens. (Courtesy of Falls W. Price.)

Sgt. Roy Donald Price, 30th Infantry Division, "Old Hickory," fought at St. Lo, where he suffered wounds in the legs. He returned to combat for the advance into Belgium. Roy Price received the Purple Heart, the Good Conduct Medal, and the EAME Campaign Medal with two Bronze Service Stars. After the war, Price (a brother of Falls W. and Arthur F. Price) opened a shoe store at the county line. He also served as clerk of court in Cleveland County for several years. (Courtesy of Beverly Manous Price.)

On December 23, 1944, Sgt. Falls Price (right) was seated in a café in Liege, Belgium. When he glanced up, he saw a soldier who looked like a larger version of the 16-year-old brother he left behind three years ago. It was indeed his brother, Cpl. Arthur Fred Price (left) of Company B, 172nd Combat Engineer Battalion. The two had a wonderful reunion and had their photographs made together. (Courtesy of Carolyn Barbee, Falls Price, and Nell Price Burns.)

The German assault all but split the Allied front. Counterattacks from the north by British Field Marshal B.L. Montgomery and southern attacks by Gen. George S. Patton stopped the Germans. Cpl. Arthur F. Price was killed on December 28, 1944, when his rifle snagged a landmine five days after the reunion with his brother Falls W. Price; he left behind his beautiful young wife and 20-month-old daughter (the co-author). (Courtesy of Carolyn Barbee, Falls Price, and Nell Price Burns [now deceased].)

Sgt. John T. Martin, Battery B, 580th Anti-Aircraft Artillery Battalion, 83rd Infantry Division, "Thunderbolts," manned a .30-caliber water-cooled machine gun. His nickname was "Pop" because he was 30 when he was drafted. His dependents were his wife Burton Blanton Martin, his son Dan, and his mother Oris Cox Martin. He participated in the Northern France, Ardennes, Rhineland, and Central Europe campaigns and suffered wounds on January 24, 1945, in the German Rhineland. He earned the Purple Heart, Combat Infantryman's Badge, the Bronze Star Medal, the EAME Campaign Medal with four Bronze Service Stars, and the Good Conduct Medal. (Courtesy of John Dan Martin.)

Sgt. William M. "Mac" Fite (left), Company I, 291st Infantry, 75th Division, participated in the Rhineland and Ardennes Campaigns. He earned the Purple Heart, the Combat Infantryman's Badge, the EAME Campaign Medal with two Bronze Service Stars, the American Campaign Service Medal, the Army of Occupation Medal (Germany), the World War II Victory Medal, the Good Conduct Medal, and the Bronze Star Medal. His brother S.Sgt. George Fite (right) served four years in England. Another brother served in the Pacific. (Courtesy of the family of Mac and George Fite.)

Cpl. George H. Shull served as a combat engineer in the 517th Parachute Regimental Combat Team. He entered combat in June 1944, just north of Rome. Shull made his first combat jump in Southern France on August 15, 1944. He suffered wounds from a landmine near Sospel, France. At the exact time of his injury, his mother rose up in bed and shouted, "George has been wounded." He recuperated in Naples for two months. For his injuries, Corporal Shull earned the Purple Heart. (Courtesy of George H. Shull.)

Cpl. George H. Shull (right) appears in Nice, France, with fellow Cleveland County native James "Jim" Botts (left, with ballglove). In December 1944, the 517th Parachute RCT, attached to the 82nd Airborne Division, "All American," participated in the Battle of the Bulge and the Rhineland and Central Europe Campaigns. Corporal Shull earned the EAME Campaign Medal with Silver Service Star and Bronze Arrowhead, the World War II Victory Medal, the Army of Occupation Medal (Germany), and the Good Conduct Medal. (Courtesy of George H. Shull.)

S.Sgt. Ralph L. Pittman, Cannon Company, 358th Infantry Regiment, 90th Infantry Division, "Tough Hombres," served as a squad leader. He participated in the Normandy, Northern France, Rhineland, Ardennes, and Central Europe Campaigns. He earned the Combat Infantryman's Badge, the EAME Campaign Medal with five Bronze Service Stars and Bronze Arrowhead, the World War II Victory Medal, and the Good Conduct Medal. Here, Sergeant Pittman makes friends with civilians in a liberated village in France. (Courtesy of Billy Seay and the family of Ralph L. Pittman.)

Second Lt. Warren J. Reid was a platoon leader for Company G, 26th Infantry Regiment, 1st Division, "Big Red One." He emphasized that "the proudest moment of my life was receiving my commission from Officer's Candidate School." At the Battle of the Bulge, he suffered wounds and had to lie in the open all day until his evacuation under the cover of darkness. He received promotion to first lieutenant in May 1945 and a discharged as a captain in July 1946. He received the Purple Heart, the EAME Campaign Medal with two Bronze Service Stars, and the World War II Victory Medal. (Courtesy of Warren J. Reid.)

PFC Thomas M. "Jack" Gardner, Company B, 503rd Military Police Battalion, performed the duties of a military policeman in the Normandy, Northern France, Ardennes, Rhineland, and Central Europe Campaigns. This 1945 photograph shows Gardner in Germany. He earned the EAME Campaign Medal with five Bronze Service Stars, the World War II Victory Medal, and the Good Conduct Medal. His unit received the Meritorious Unit Commendation. (Courtesy of Jack Gardner and Ned Cash.)

Sgt. Thomas M. Ballew, 231st AAA Searchlight Battalion, sailed for England on the SS *Explorer*; from England he went to France on an LST. His unit participated in the capture of Cherbourg, France. Sergeant Ballew served as S2 Intelligence Clerk. (Courtesy of Thomas M. Ballew.)

At war's end Sgt. Thomas M. Ballew received his discharge from Headquarters Company, 417th Signal Battalion, 9th Air Force. He earned the American Theater Campaign Medal, the EAME Campaign Medal with Service Stars, and the Good Conduct Medal. (Courtesy of Thomas M. Ballew.)

The family of Cpl. John A. Parker received notice that he had been missing in action since June 9, 1944. The War Department confirmed his death on June 21, 1944. John and his wife Jean had been married in the fall of 1941. He entered service in November 1941 and had been overseas 22 months. Corporal Parker's death occurred while he was serving in the European Theater of Operations. His Purple Heart was posthumous. (Courtesy of Judith Parker-Proctor.)

Seven

Pacific and Atlantic (1941–1945)

A Two-Ocean Navy

The naval battle in the Atlantic Ocean presented the U.S. Atlantic Fleet with the challenge of helping the Royal Navy to defeat the German submarine menace. Defeat of the U-boats would allow the Allies to move vital supplies and millions of troops—vital steps for the defeat of Adolf Hitler. These sailors overcame the "wolf packs" and the fierce storms of the North Atlantic Ocean. The navy's ultimate success freed Europe. After the attack on Pearl Harbor, the U.S. Pacific Fleet faced the well-trained and hard-fighting Japanese Imperial Fleet. Using every type of ship, from the smallest landing craft to the far-ranging carrier task forces, the U.S. Navy battled the implacable foe. By September 1945, the fleet, under command of fighting admirals like William F. Halsey Jr., Raymond A. Spruance, and Marc A. Mitscher, had defeated the Japanese.

The USS *La Vallette* was a Fletcher-class destroyer launched in June 21, 1942. Serving as a plank owner (original crew member) was Gunner's Mate 2c. Charlie Dewitt Stephens. The *La Vallette* first saw combat on January 29, 1943, at Guadalcanal, where it shot down three Japanese aircraft. (Courtesy of Roger and Jerry Stephens.)

On January 30, 1943, while screening the USS *Chicago*, the USS *La Vallette* shot down 6 "Betty" bombers, but it received a torpedo hit that killed 22 crewmen. This strike necessitated repairs in Espiritu Santo, New Hebrides. The ship sailed to Mare Island Naval Yard for full repairs and returned to the Pacific. On board was Gunner's Mate Charlie Stephens. (Courtesy of Roger and Jerry Stephens.)

Gunner's Mate Charlie Stephens fondly remembered the ship's mascot, "Boots." Boots served aboard the *La Vallette* the entire time that the ship was in commission. On the nights of October 1 and 2, 1943, the *La Vallette*'s crew contacted Japanese troop barges off Kolombangara in the Solomons; the *La Vallette* sank four barges and damaged two. The crew awarded Boots the Asiatic Pacific Campaign Medal with nine Bronze Service Stars, the Philippine Liberation Ribbon, the EAME Campaign Medal, and "many, many more." (Courtesy of Roger and Jerry Stephens.)

Gunner's Mate Charlie Stephens (center) and fellow crewmen A.B. Jackson (left) and John Brazzil (right) participated in the Battle of Leyte Gulf. On Valentine's Day 1945, the *La Vallette* received extensive damage while minesweeping in Marieveles Harbor. The mine killed 6 and wounded 23, including Stephens, who earned the Purple Heart, the EAME Campaign Medal with Bronze Service Star, the American Defense Service Medal, the Asiatic Pacific Campaign Medal with seven Bronze Service Stars, and the Philippine Liberation Ribbon with two Bronze Service Stars. (Courtesy of Roger and Jerry Stephens.)

S1c. William Buck Goforth served aboard five ships, including USS *Briareus* (a cargo ship). He was at Eniwetok Atoll; the Ulithi Atoll, the staging area for the invasion of the Philippines; Leyte Gulf; Okinawa; and Japan. Seaman Goforth suffered injury near the Japanese coast when the 36-foot boat he was piloting hit a buoy. (Courtesy of Mrs. Frances Pilgrim and William Buck Goforth.)

A fond memory of S1c. William Buck Goforth was meeting with his father, Fireman 1c. Claud Paul Goforth (seated on rock), who was serving aboard the USS *Texas*. Their unexpected reunion was near Okinawa. (Courtesy of William Buck Goforth.)

S1c. A.C. "Tom" Parker served in the 1st Division aboard the USS *Mackinac* and was part of the 3rd Fleet. The *Mackinac* resupplied seaplanes with men, fuel, and ordnance. He served as a boatswain when necessary. His battle station was at a quad-40mm gun. On the quarterdeck of the ship is a Christmas tree erected by the crew. (Courtesy of A.C. "Tom" Parker.)

During his time in service, S1c. A.C. "Tom" Parker participated in operations at Saipan and Iwo Jima; in the invasion of Okinawa, where the *Mackinac* had to evade a Kamikaze; and at the surrender at Tokyo Bay in September 1945. He received the American Campaign Medal, the Asiatic Pacific Campaign Medal with two Bronze Service Stars, the World War II Victory Medal, and the Occupation Medal (Japan). (Courtesy of A.C. "Tom" Parker.)

S1c. (RM) William C. Howington served with U.S. LCT Flotilla 19, LCT Group 123, and LCT 595. His duties included service in England, France, and the South Pacific. He earned the American Theater Campaign Medal, the EAME Campaign Medal, and the World War II Victory Medal. His brothers include Hoyt B. Howington (U.S. Army), Nolan P. Howington (U.S. Army), Hal W. Howington (U.S. Army), and Hugh Q. Howington (U.S. Army). (Courtesy of the Howington Family.)

Coxswain Hubert Lee Greene entered service on June 17, 1944, and served aboard the USS *Knudson*, a high-speed transport, in the Pacific. He earned the American Campaign Medal, the Asiatic Pacific Campaign Medal with two Bronze Service Stars, and the World War II Victory Medal. (Courtesy of Reta May.)

S1c. Grady Flay Walker served in the U.S. Navy from September 25, 1943, until March 30, 1946, aboard LST 516 and LSM 110. He participated in Normandy, where his ship transported men and equipment to the beaches and evacuated casualties back to England. Walker earned the Army of Occupation Medal (Japan) along with the EAME Campaign Medal with a Bronze Service Star, the World War II Victory Medal, and the Good Conduct Medal. (Courtesy of Grady Flay Walker.)

Electrician's Mate 2c. Fred Union Teague served aboard the USS *Springer*, a Balao-class submarine. He conducted his first patrol off Naha, Okinawa, where the *Springer* sank at least two ships—one carrying eight Kaiten midget submarines. In the second patrol, the *Springer* sank a Japanese destroyer and survived 27 Japanese depth charges in the counterattack. He received the American Theater Campaign Medal, the Asiatic Pacific Campaign Medal with one Bronze Service Star, and the World War II Victory Medal. (Courtesy of Fred Union Teague.)

Aviation Mechanic's Mate 3c. John Levi Whitener (third from left) served in Florida, California, and Vanibru, Okinawa. While stationed at Okinawa, his crew flew postwar missions into Japan and China. He earned the Asiatic Pacific Campaign Medal with two Bronze Service Stars, the World War II Victory Medal, and the Good Conduct Medal. (Courtesy of John Levi Whitener.)

Aviation Ordnanceman 3c. Carl Dudley Whitaker began active duty in the U.S. Navy on May 17, 1944, upon graduation from Mooresboro High School. He served at the naval air stations in Jacksonville, Vero Beach, and Miami during World War II. Carl Dudley Whitaker served also during the Korean War; his services during the Korean War included duty upon the fleet carriers USS *Valley Forge* and the USS *Philippine Sea.* He had two children and five grandchildren. (Courtesy of Nellene Jones Whitaker.)

Sonarman 3c. Don Hugh Ellis Sr. served aboard the USS *Dobler*, a destroyer escort assigned to anti-submarine patrols in the Atlantic. Ellis received reassignment as Interior Communications Electrician's Mate 2c. aboard the USS *Valley Forge*. He received his discharge in December 1947. He earned the American Theater Campaign Medal and the Asiatic Pacific Campaign Medal. (Courtesy of Carolyn Shrader and Susan Collier.)

Lt. (jg) Earl Holleman Meacham commanded the guncrew aboard the USS *Argentina* and the motor vessel *Cape Uga*. He was also a port director liaison officer in Southend-on-Sea, United Kingdom. During transport duty in 1943, the *Argentina* transported POWs from North Africa to England. He and his friend Italian officer Giovanni Bertoldi reunited in 1965 in Rome. He retired as a lieutenant commander and earned the American Theater Campaign Medal, the EAME Campaign Medal, and the Asiatic Pacific Campaign Medal. His 18-month-old daughter (page 115) loved wearing a uniform like her dad. (Courtesy of Lacy Meacham Ballard.)

S1c. Odus Erastus Lee Jr. served aboard the USS *Eisele*, which escorted convoys between the Gilbert and Marshall Islands and Pearl Harbor. The ship continued its escort duties in the Marianas and supported operations at Palau, the Philippines, and Okinawa. Seaman Lee received the American Theater Campaign Medal, the Asiatic Pacific Campaign Medal with one Bronze Service Star, the Philippine Liberation Medal, the World War II Victory Medal, and the Good Conduct Medal. (Courtesy of the family of Odus Erastus Lee Jr.)

Boatswain Mate 2c. Kenneth Porter Crotts served aboard the USS *Fomalhaut*, an attack transport that participated at Guadalcanal and the Northern Solomons. By late 1944, Crotts was serving on the USS *Ozark*. He participated in the invasion of Luzon at Lingayen Gulf, Iwo Jima, and Okinawa. He earned the American Theater Campaign Medal, the Asiatic Pacific with four Bronze Service Stars, the World War II Victory Medal, and the Good Conduct Medal. (Courtesy of Ned Cash and the family of Kenneth Porter Crotts.)

S1c. Clyde Lee Camp served aboard the USS *Rosemont*, the USS *Charles*, the USS *Roger Griswold*, and the USS *Miaoulis*. Clyde received the American Theater Campaign Medal, the World War II Victory Medal, and the Good Conduct Medal. Four of his brothers also served. Pictured are, from left to right, Lawrence (U.S. Navy), Clyde (U.S. Navy), Charlie M. Camp (father), Everette (U.S. Army), Etta McCurry Camp (mother), Ralph (U.S. Navy), and Badge (U.S. Navy). (Courtesy of Everette Camp.)

Sonarman 3c. Peter Ferreira (right) served on the USS *Tingey* in the Pacific as part of the 3rd and 5th Fleets. He recalls normal activities such as refueling at sea, performing anti-submarine patrols, transferring rescued pilots back to their aircraft carriers, and enduring the great typhoons. He was told by a battleship sailor that during one typhoon all that was visible of the *Tingey* was "its radar mast sweeping around." He is pictured with a Brazilian sailor in Key West in 1944. (Courtesy of Peter Ferreira.)

On February 19, 1945, the USS *Tingey* rescued 72 sailors off the carrier *Franklin*, damaged by a Japanese bomber crashing on its deck off Okinawa. Sonarman 3c. Peter Ferreira remembers distinctly that the *Tingey* made several rescue attempts; they buried 17 men at sea. This photo shows Peter and his wife Jeannette Lemieux on their 1945 wedding day. He earned the American Theater Campaign Medal, the Asiatic Pacific Campaign Medal with two Bronze Service Stars, the Philippine Liberation Medal, and the World War II Victory Medal. (Courtesy of Peter Ferreira.)

Chief Fire Controlman Billy Depriest entered service on December 6, 1936, and served aboard the USS *Wyoming*. Depriest's wartime service was aboard the USS *Rowan*, as part of the invasions of North Africa, Sicily, and Salerno. On the night of September 10, 1943, the *Rowan* suffered a torpedo attack. The ship sank within seconds; 273 men died, but Depriest was one of 70 survivors. Here he (right) relaxes with Jim Forrester of Spindale, North Carolina. (Courtesy of Billy Depriest.)

Chief Fire Controlman Billy Depriest ended the war assigned to the Naval Gun Factory in Washington, D.C. Depriest received the Purple Heart, the American Theater Campaign Medal, the EAME Campaign Medal with three Bronze Service Stars, the Good Conduct Medal. This 1936 Norfolk Naval Boot Camp photograph shows Depriest standing with rifle in right hand on the far left of the second row. (Courtesy of Billy Depriest.)

Coxswain Thomas Eli Rich entered the U.S. Navy on September 9, 1943. He would serve two years and five months. His duty stations included the Naval Air Station Brunswick, Maine, and the NAAS Casco Bay, Maine, where he served as a crew member of a PT boat; his PT patrolled the North Atlantic as a defense against enemy submarines. He earned the American Theater Campaign Medal and the World War II Victory Medal. (Courtesy of his brother Charles E. Rich.)

John Herndon Mitchem served in a medical unit in Texas during World War II. His two sons, William "Sam" Presley Mitchem and Ralph Mitchem, also served in the war. (Courtesy of Sam Mitchem and Rachel Tanner.)

William "Sam" Presley Mitchem served in a fighter squadron in Florida. He also served in the Coast Guard. He is pictured here with his wife, Frances. (Courtesy of Sam Mitchem and Rachel Tanner.)

Ralph Mitchem served on an aircraft carrier. He had played professional baseball before the war. He was wounded when his carrier was struck. After the war, he served as umpire in the minor leagues. He is pictured with his wife, Ruth, and baby daughter, Linda. Little Linda died at about age 6. (Courtesy of Sam Mitchem and Rachel Tanner.)

Loyd Sewell Barnett was recruited into the naval reserve from Appalachian State Teachers College. He saw Frank Sinatra, Benny Goodman, Tommy Dorsey, and others while at midshipman's school in New York. On April 8, 1944, he reported on board the USS *Doyle*. For his services Lt. (jg) Loyd Sewell Barnett received the American Theater Campaign Medal, the Asiatic Pacific Campaign Medal, the EAME Campaign Medal with two Bronze Service Stars, and the World War II Victory Medal. (Courtesy of Joyce Barnett Culbreth.)

The *Doyle* used its 5-inch guns to provide fire support for the "Fox Green" section of Omaha Beach. The *Doyle* was as close as 1,000 yards from the beach and fired 558 rounds during the mission. As assistant gunnery officer, Barnett said, "We fired at anything that moved." He recalled that the night before the Normandy Invasion, a British radio station played "the saddest music he had ever heard." This photograph shows troops storming ashore from an LCI landing craft. (Courtesy of the U.S. Coast Guard.)

By 1945, a combination of sea and air power defined the United States Navy. The above photograph shows the aircraft carrier *Ticonderoga* preceding the USS *Washington*, the USS *North Carolina*, and the USS *South Dakota*; these ships, and other ships of the fleet, left devastation in their wake. (Courtesy of the U.S. Navy.)

The photo above shows Adm. William F. Halsey's 3rd Fleet anchored in Sagami Wan, in sight of Mt. Fuji in late August 1945. Within days, the fleet would move to Tokyo Bay for the final surrender. (Courtesy of the U.S. Navy.)

Eight

Germany, the Rhineland, and the Surrender (1945)

Prevailing in Europe

The year 1945 began with the defeat of the last German counteroffensive in the west. With the crossing of the Rhine River in March 1945, the Allies advanced across Germany to the Elbe River. In the east, the Soviet Union's Red Army stood on the Oder River poised to attack Berlin.

After crossing the Rhine in March 1945, American Armed Forces pursued the decimated foe. William A. "Gus" Rich, 116th Ordnance Medium Maintenance Company, 3rd Army, served as a .50-caliber machine gunner on an M-4 Sherman tank. Rich photographed his fellow crewmen proudly displaying a captured Nazi flag during the advance of 1945. This vehicle has appliquéd armor plates. (Courtesy of Charles E. Rich.)

Cpl. William A. "Gus" Rich served in the 116th Ordnance Medium Maintenance Company, 3rd Army. He served in the European Theatre from January 8, 1945, until the end of World War II. He and his unit participated in the Ardennes, Rhineland, and Central Europe Campaigns. He earned the EAME Campaign Medal with three Bronze Service Stars and the World War II Victory Medal. Rich is pictured here with his M-2 .50-caliber machine gun. (Courtesy of Charles E. Rich.)

Capt. Nolan P. Howington served as regimental chaplain of the 273rd Infantry Regiment of the 69th Infantry Division, "Fighting 69th." He participated in the Rhineland and Central Europe Campaigns. He was among the first soldiers to meet troops of the Soviet Red Army at the Elbe River in Germany. Chaplain Howington earned the Bronze Star Medal and the EAME Campaign Medal with two Bronze Service Stars. His brothers Hal (page 12, 67), Hoyt (page 67, 113), Hugh (page 54, 67), and William (page 67) also served. (Courtesy of William C. Howington.)

Three days after Pearl Harbor, James Edwin Smith and 124 other boys from Cleveland County traveled by bus to Fort Jackson, South Carolina, to join the army. Smith received assignment to Battery C, 182nd Field Artillery Battalion, as a .50-caliber machine gunner. Eighteen other local boys received assignment to the other three batteries of the battalion. Cpl. James Edwin Smith (right) and his father William Weaver Smith (left) of the Sharon community pose when Edwin came home on furlough in 1943. (Courtesy of James Edwin Smith.)

After crossing to England, Cpl. James Edwin Smith and his unit went ashore on Utah Beach on June 17 (D+11). His saddest memory is seeing a dead German soldier with his hands crossed upon his chest and folded as if he were praying. He recalls two-foot-deep snow, soldiers so badly frostbitten they lost toes and feet, being strafed by German jet fighters, and the Dachau Concentration Camp. James Edwin Smith posed in England for this photograph. (Courtesy of James Edwin Smith.)

Cleveland County men who served with Cpl. James Edwin Smith were Pat Patterson, Bill Leonard, Clyde Bridges, Irwin Champion, Clyde Rogers, L.D. Reynolds, Clifton McSwain, Leon Harris, Haskell Beam, Walter Putnam, Joe Depriest Sr., Joe Davis, Jim Allen, Charles Goodman, A.T. Newton, Crete Putnam, and Colon McSwain. Smith thanks Almighty God for bringing him home and recalls how thankful he is that he served his country. Smith received the EAME Campaign Medal with five Bronze Service Stars and the Battle of the Bulge Commemorative Medal. (Courtesy of James Edwin Smith.)

During a seven-day ocean crossing on the *Queen Mary* to Glasgow, Scotland, most of the men became deathly ill after a breakfast of kidney stew. The Thanksgiving Day trip home in 1945 was harrowing; a dreadful storm lasted all the way across the Atlantic. "The ship drifted backwards 100 miles from Boston Harbor, and the men wore their life jackets." The ship docked on Pearl Harbor Day. Smith was "welcomed home with open arms and a brand new easy chair." (Courtesy of James Edwin Smith and Harold W. Hayes.)

Cpl. George Clyde Rogers, 182nd Field Artillery Battalion, served as a forward gun observer relaying messages by jeep from headquarters to the artillery. During World War II, the battalion fired 58,229 rounds. Rogers participated in the Normandy, Northern France, Rhineland, and Central Europe Campaigns and served with fellow Cleveland County resident James Edwin Smith. (Courtesy of G.A. Rogers.)

Also serving in the army was George Clyde Rogers's brother, Emmitt Harvey Rogers. Emmitt Harvey Rogers served as a cook in a medical detachment at Fort Jackson, South Carolina. (Courtesy of G.A. Rogers.)

Another of the Rogers brothers was Ernest Lloyd Rogers. Ernest Lloyd served in the United States Marine Corps. (Courtesy of G.A. Rogers.)

Hal Reid Haynes was reared in Kings Mountain, North Carolina. He was the youngest of William Columbus and Brentie Weaver Haynes's 10 children. He was born February 18, 1927, and died January 20, 1949. Even though he was very young during World War II, he served his country. During the Korean War, he served in the 82nd Airborne Division in Europe. (Courtesy of niece Rachel Haynes Tanner.)

While serving in Company L, 8th Infantry Regiment, 4th Infantry Division, "Ivy," PFC Arthur R. Ledbetter received the Bronze Star Medal for "exemplary conduct in ground combat against the armed enemy." Ledbetter participated in the Normandy, Northern France, Rhineland, and Central Europe Campaigns. He suffered wounds from artillery on September 27, 1944. He earned the Purple Heart, the Combat Infantryman's Badge, the EAME Campaign Medal with four Bronze Service Stars, and the World War II Victory Medal. (Courtesy of Arthur R. Ledbetter.)

Sgt. Robert Cuthrell was a replacement assigned to Company M, 23rd Infantry Regiment, 28th Infantry Division, "Keystone." He was in a heavy weapons company in Central Europe; they used .50-caliber machine guns and mortars. For his services he received the EAME Campaign Medal and the Army of Occupation (Germany); his unit earned the French Croix de Guerre Fourrageres. (Courtesy of Robert Cuthrell.)

Cpl. A.V. Lanier was in the Anti-Tank Company of the 397th Infantry Regiment, 100th Division, "Century." He drove trucks in the Rhineland and Central Europe Campaigns. He twice suffered wounds: on December 10, 1944, in France and on April 12, 1945, in Germany. Corporal Lanier received the Purple Heart with Oak Leaf Cluster, the American Theater Service Medal, the EAME Campaign Medal, the World War II Victory Medal, and the Good Conduct Medal. (Courtesy of the family of A.V. Lanier.)

T5g. John B. Morgan drove trucks with Headquarters Company, 2nd Battalion, 398th Infantry Regiment, 100th Division. He fought at the Battle of the Bulge, the Vosges Mountains, La Salle, Bitche, Heilbronn, and the occupation of Stuttgart. He earned the Bronze Star Medal, the EAME Campaign Medal with two Bronze Service Stars, the Meritorious Service Medal, the World War II Victory Medal, the Good Conduct Medal, and the Combat Infantryman's Badge. (Courtesy of the family of John B. Morgan.)

S.Sgt. John Davis Fisher served in the United States Navy from November 1, 1945, until October 1, 1947. He re-enlisted in the United States Air Force from April 1, 1951, until September 1, 1953. He served as a military police office in France. (Courtesy of Catherine Fisher Spangler.)

PFC John Leon Wortman, Company B, 330th Infantry Regiment, 83rd Infantry Division, "Thunderbolts," recalls that "men froze to death at the Bulge." He met the Red Army at the Elbe on a pontoon bridge. Wortman entered the service after graduating from Lattimore High School. He earned the Combat Infantryman's Badge, the EAME Campaign Medal with three Bronze Service Stars, the World War II Victory Medal, the Army of Occupation Medal (Germany), and the Good Conduct Medal. (Courtesy of John L. Wortman.)

PFC John L "Johnie" Lattimore, 92nd Armored Field Artillery Battalion, 2nd Armored Division, "Hell on Wheels," V Corps, endured a bout of blood poisoning and a debilitating back injury in the North African Invasion. He elected to remain with his unit rather than return home. Lattimore participated in Normandy, Northern France, Ardennes, Rhineland, and Central Europe Campaigns and earned the EAME Campaign Medal with five Bronze Service Stars, the World War II Victory Medal, the Army of Occupation (Germany) Medal, and the Belgian Fourrageres. (Courtesy of Charles L. Elliott.)

William Odell Lovelace served in an army infantry unit. He participated in the Battle of the Bulge and in both the Rhineland and Central Europe Campaigns. He was born on April 24, 1913, which means he was one of the older men in his unit. (Courtesy of Edna L. Cooper.)

S.Sgt. Marion O. Morehead drove a tank in Company C, 48th Armored Infantry Battalion, 6th Armored Division, "Super Sixth." He recalled the hedgerows of France, how cold it was in the Ardennes with no heat in the vehicle, and his concern at losing a track in the Battle of the Bulge. For his services he earned the Bronze Star, the EAME Campaign Medal with five Bronze Service Stars, and the Good Conduct Medal. (Courtesy of Ned Cash.)

PFC Horace A. Fox served as a military policeman in Company C, 62nd Armored Infantry Battalion, 14th Armored Division, "Liberators." He was one of the younger participants, and he served overseas six months. His wife recalls that he spent his 19th birthday guarding German prisoners in an old barn. His unit liberated prisoners from camps in the area. He received the EAME Campaign Medal with one Bronze Service Star, the World War II Victory Medal, and the Good Conduct Medal. (Courtesy of Nell C. Fox.)

T4g. Charles H. Ledbetter (second from right, standing), Company A, 1258th Engineer Combat Battalion, Third Army, served as a 2 1/2–ton truck driver. He participated in the Rhineland, Ardennes, and Central Europe Campaigns. At Mainz, crossing the Rhine, his unit constructed the longest tactical floating bridge—1,896 feet—of the war; it was here that Lt. Gen. George S. Patton "marked his territory." (Courtesy of Margie W. Ledbetter.)

T4g. Charles H. Ledbetter's unit helped liberate Dachau Concentration Camp. Ledbetter (third from right) was one of five brothers who served: Sgt. Carl served with the infantry, Claude was a truck driver in the artillery and participated in the Normandy Invasion, Sidney was a half-track driver and was wounded in action, and Morris served in Korea and postwar Germany. Charles earned the EAME Campaign Medal with three Bronze Service Stars, the World War II Victory Medal, and the Army of Occupation Medal (Germany). (Courtesy of Margie W. Ledbetter.)

PFC James O. Harris served as a tank gunner with the 2nd Calvary Reconnaissance Squadron, "Patton's Ghosts." He recalls with pride how the tanks of the 2nd Calvary broke down the gates of Stalag IXB at Bad Orb, Germany, and liberated nearly 6,000 Allied prisoners of war. More than 3,000 were Americans, many from the 106th Infantry Division. (Courtesy of James O. Harris.)

PFC James O. Harris participated in the Normandy, Northern France, Ardennes, Rhineland, and Central Europe Campaigns. He earned the EAME Campaign Medal with five Bronze Service Stars. (Courtesy of James O. Harris.)

T5g. Carl Clifford Hughes, Company B, 3rd Tank Battalion, 6th Armored Division, "Super Sixth," entered service in March 1942 and served until October 1945. In his nine months of combat, he participated in the Normandy, Northern France, Rhineland, Ardennes, and Central Europe Campaigns. Hughes won the Bronze Star. For his services he earned the EAME Campaign Medal with five Bronze Service Stars, the World War II Victory Medal, and the Good Conduct Medal. (Courtesy of C. Clifford Hughes.)

In 1943, T5g. William Keever Hamrick, 363rd Quartermaster Service Company had Burton-on-Trent in the English Midlands as his duty station. His unit attached to the 531st Special Engineer Brigade for the D-Day Landings. On D+2, Technician Hamrick went ashore on Omaha Beach to support the advance of the 1st Infantry Division. He received the EAME Campaign Medal with five Bronze Service Stars and Bronze Arrowhead, the World War II Victory Medal, and the Good Conduct Medal. (Courtesy of William Keever Hamrick.)

William Keever Hamrick supplied this photograph. Hamrick's unit had remained in the beachhead for six months before relocating to Liege, Belgium. The last stop for this unit was Furth, Germany. Upon his return to Cleveland County, he went to see his grandfather. When Keever had left for war, his grandfather was sitting on the porch and had said, "Let's see what kind of man the service makes out of you." When Keever got home, his grandfather was on the porch and said, "Well, son, they made a man out of you." (Courtesy of William Keever Hamrick.)

PFC Colon Martin Melton, 87th Mountain Infantry Regiment, 10th Mountain Division, "Mountaineers," entered service on April 14, 1944. He served as a heavy machine gunner in the Northern Apennines and Po Valley Campaigns in Italy before his discharge on November 30, 1945. He earned for his services the EAME Campaign Medal with two Bronze Service Stars, the Combat Infantryman's Badge, the World War II Victory Medal, and the Good Conduct Medal. (Courtesy of Colon M. Melton.)

Pictured here is PFC Colon Martin Melton (driver) driving two ski troopers to the slopes near the Swiss border. A spring thaw had come to the area in April 1945, however, and the troopers were unable to ski because of the soft snow. (Courtesy of Colon Martin Melton.)

Sgt. Paul G. Mashburn (right) commanded an M-5 Stuart tank in Headquarters Company, 38th Armored Infantry Battalion, 7th Armored Division, "Lucky Seventh." In December 1944, while scouting ahead of his unit, Mashburn's tank became stuck in a marsh. The crew disabled the vehicle; they were moving away when German troops supported by a Tiger tank surrounded them. A burp gun shot Mashburn through the right leg. He became a POW for five months and weighed only 103 pounds at his liberation. (Courtesy of Paul Mashburn.)

S.Sgt. Ward Randolph, Company B, 38th Infantry Regiment, 2nd Infantry Division, "Indianhead," died in action on April 15, 1945, in Germany. Sergeant Randolph participated in the Central Europe Campaign. (Courtesy of Douglas Hayes.)

The grave marker of S.Sgt. Ward Randolph reads: "He gave his life for his country in Germany. He is not dead. He is just asleep." He earned the Purple Heart, a posthumous Bronze Star Medal, a posthumous Combat Infantryman's Badge, the EAME, and the World War II Victory Medal. (Courtesy of Douglas Hayes.)

T5g. J.E. Blanton, Battery A, 627th Field Artillery Battalion, received assignment in April 1945 to the 106th Infantry Division, "Golden Lions," for the Central Europe Campaign. He served as an automobile mechanic. He remained in Germany for 13 months and served in the Army of Occupation (Germany). For his services he earned the EAME Campaign Medal with one Bronze Service Stars, the World War II Victory Medal, and the Good Conduct Medal. He qualified as a sharpshooter with a .30-caliber rifle. (Courtesy of J.E. Blanton.)

Sgt. Carl Blanton, 325th Combat Engineers, 100th Division, "Century," was a construction foreman supervising a crew of 12 combat engineers. Prior to his military service, he had two years at Gardner-Webb College. He earned the American Campaign Medal, the EAME Campaign Medal with Bronze Service Star, the World War II Victory Medal, and the Good Conduct Medal. He qualified as a sharpshooter with a .30-caliber rifle and as a marksman with a machine gun. (Courtesy of Carl Blanton.)

Sgt. Carl Blanton (center) stands with his brothers in front of a Nazi flag. Carl's unit received a Presidential Unit Citation. Calus Blanton (left) was killed in Vietnam as a civilian. J.Y. Blanton (right) was wounded while serving in the infantry. (Courtesy of Carl Blanton.)

Elbert C. Costner, Company E, 47th Infantry Regiment, 9th Infantry Division, "Old Reliables," carried a BAR. He landed on Utah Beach on D+2. Costner suffered wounds on June 22, 1944, from a grenade and a mortar-shell fragment. He participated in the Rhineland and Central Europe Campaigns. He earned two Purple Hearts, the Bronze Star, the EAME Campaign Medal with four Bronze Service Stars, the Combat Infantryman's Badge, and the World War II Victory Medal. His unit received the Presidential Unit Citation. (Courtesy of Elbert C. Costner.)

T5g. Clay D. Wilson, Company B, 17th Armored Engineer Battalion, 2nd Armored Division, "Hell on Wheels," served as a heavy truck driver during the Normandy, Northern France, Ardennes, Rhineland, and Central Europe Campaigns. He earned the EAME Campaign Medal with five Bronze Service Stars and the Good Conduct Medal. He qualified as a sharpshooter with a .30-caliber rifle and a marksman with a .30-caliber carbine. (Courtesy of Clay D. Wilson and Ned Cash.)

PFC Osborne R. McGinnis was a gunner in Company C, 331st Infantry Regiment, 83rd Infantry Division, "Thunderbolts." He participated in Ardennes, Rhineland, and the Central Europe Campaigns. Even though he had five dependents, he was drafted and served overseas 10 months. He earned the Combat Infantryman's Badge, the EAME Campaign Medal with three Bronze Service Stars, the World War II Victory Medal, and the Good Conduct Medal; he was a sharpshooter with a .30-caliber rifle. (Courtesy of Frances Morgan.)

T5g. Elbert K. McSwain drove trucks for Headquarters Company, 7th Armored Group. He participated in the Normandy, Northern France, Rhineland, and Central Europe Campaigns. He received the American Theater Campaign Medal, the EAME Campaign Medal with four Bronze Service Stars, the World War II Victory Medal, and the Good Conduct Medal. McSwain (left) is pictured aboard ship wearing his life-vest. (Courtesy of Teala McSwain.)

T4g. John William Beheler, 78th Financial Dispersing Section, 3rd Army Headquarters, participated in Normandy, Northern France, Ardennes, Rhineland, and Central Europe Campaigns. Beheler recalls that while he was at the Battle of the Bulge, even though they were wearing heavy-weather gear, many of the men suffered frostbite. Pictured here at the rear of a 2 1/2–ton truck is Beheler (third from left). (Courtesy of John W. Beheler.)

T4g. John William Beheler survived a shipwreck in the North Atlantic during his time in service. For his services he earned the EAME Campaign Medal with Five Bronze Service Stars and the Good Conduct Medal. He qualified as a marksman with a .30-caliber rifle. (Courtesy of John W. Beheler.)

S.Sgt. David H. Prince served as a cannoneer on a 57-mm anti-tank gun in the Anti-Tank Company, 310th Infantry Regiment, 78th Division, "Lightning Division." He participated in the Ardennes, Rhineland and Central Europe Campaigns. He suffered wounds on February 6, 1945. He earned the Purple Heart, the Combat Infantryman's Badge, the American Defense Service Medal, the EAME Campaign Medal with three Bronze Service Stars, the World War II Victory Medal, and the Good Conduct Medal. Dr. David H. Prince later taught at Wofford College. (Courtesy of David H. Prince.)

Cpl. Thomas Luther Peace was a radio repairman in Company H, 398th Infantry Regiment, 100th Division, "Century." He participated in the Central Europe Campaign and, after the end of the war, served six months in occupied Germany with the 504th Military Police Battalion. He earned the EAME Campaign Medal with one Bronze Service Star, the World War II Victory Medal, the Army of Occupation (Germany), and the Good Conduct Medal. (Courtesy of Thomas Luther Peace and family.)

T4g. James Dewitt Gettys served in the 756th Engineer Parts Supply Company, 9th Armored Division, "Phantom." His most vivid memory was leaving his wife Vera Swofford Gettys and their six-month-old child when he went in service on October 11, 1944. He and his unit participated in the Battle of the Bulge, where he saw action at Trois Vierges, Luxembourg; the Remagen Bridge; and Limburg, Germany, where they liberated many prisoners of war. (Courtesy of James Dewitt Gettys.)

T4g. James Dewitt Gettys recalled being in Wurzburg, Germany, on April 12, 1945, when he heard of the death of President Roosevelt. He earned the Bronze Star Medal, the American Theater Campaign Medal, the EAME Campaign Medal with two Bronze Service Stars, the Combat Infantryman's Badge, the World War II Victory Medal, the Army of Occupation Medal (Germany), and the Good Conduct Medal. (Courtesy of James Dewitt Gettys.)

William L. Walker (left) was drafted from Gardner-Webb College in 1943. The draft notice resulted in a 21-year career in the army for Bill; he retired with the rank of warrant officer. Lt. Gen. George S. Patton personally selected Walker as his military aide. Walker summed up the man as "my idol of a general." During the Battle of the Bulge, Walker's mother sent him several cans of tenderloin meat; the Germans attacked, and he had to leave his canned goods behind. (Courtesy of William L. Walker.)

With the end of World War II, William L. Walker attended a German language and counterintelligence school in southern Germany. This photograph shows Walker with his hunt trophy: a wild boar. (Courtesy of William L. Walker.)

After duty in Germany, William L. Walker served as a regimental training officer with the 82nd Airborne. He served two years in Korea with the 24th Infantry Division, "Victory." Among his many awards are the Bronze Star, the Master Parachute Badge for 187 jumps, the Combat Infantryman's Badge, the World War II Victory Medal, the Army of Occupation (Germany), the Good Conduct Medal, the French Croix de Guerre, the Belgian Fourrageres, and the Presidential Unit Citation. (Courtesy of William L. Walker.)

T4g. James Wyatt Martin entered service on January 18, 1942, and received his discharge on November 9, 1945. He served 15 months as an automobile parts clerk and 20 months as a barber, probably because he had owned and operated his own shop before the war. He served in the European Theater, and his service helped to maintain the morale of the servicemen. (Courtesy of David J. Martin.)

Pvt. Alvin Hoyt Whitaker did basic training at Fort Hood, Texas. While he was in Texas, he served with Allen Jolley and Ned Simmons; they were all from the Lattimore-Mooresboro area. He developed a very serious case of diabetes and received his discharge before going overseas. (Courtesy of Gary Whitaker.)

Nine

Iwo Jima, Okinawa, and the Surrender of Japan (1945)

Ending the War

From the newly established air bases in the Marianas Islands, B-29 Superfortress bombers conducted numerous raids on the Japanese home islands. The purpose of these raids was to break the will of the Japanese people and their rulers. To secure an emergency landing facility, the U.S. Marine V Amphibious Corps began on February 19, 1945, a 36-day campaign to conquer the island of Iwo Jima. The resulting battle was the most famous one of World War II.

The photo above shows the 4th Marine Division coming ashore from landing crafts onto the black sands of Iwo Jima. (Courtesy of the United States Marines Corps.)

Cpl. Olen Odus Ledford, United States Marine Corps, served as a cook. He participated in the invasion of Okinawa from May 27, 1945, until July 2, 1945. He recalled to his wife how on one occasion he jumped into a foxhole, pulled a dead marine on top of him, and heard the Japanese bayonet the body over him. He finally was able to escape. Ledford was wounded by shrapnel as he crossed a field. (Courtesy of Katie L. Cook.)

T5g. Ambrose R. Cook drove trucks for the H&S Company, 46th Engineer Construction Battalion, during the occupation of Japan. His station was near Mount Fuji. He earned the World War II Victory Medal, the Army of Occupation (Japan) Medal, the American Theater Campaign Medal, the Asiatic Pacific Campaign Medal with two Bronze Service Stars, and the Good Conduct Medal. He qualified as a sharpshooter with the rifle. (Courtesy of Katie L. Cook.)

Cpl. Milbern Ward Sweezy, Pioneer Battalion, 5th Marine Division, worked both as a carpenter and a stevedore for his unit. During the Occupation of Japan, his station was near Sasebo, Japan. (Courtesy of Milbern Ward Sweezy.)

In January 1946, Cpl. Milbern Ward Sweezy received a transfer to Tientsin, China. The city was served by the seaport of Tangku. This photo, self-described as "Three Hard Heads in Tangku," shows Sweezy (in the middle) with two fellow marines. Sweezy earned the Good Conduct Medal and the Army of Occupation (Japan) Medal. (Courtesy of Milbern Ward Sweezy.)

T5g. William D. Gold served as a cook with the 82nd Chemical Mortar Battalion for 11 months while stationed in Japan. Technician Gold was responsible for planning and preparing meals; he also had the responsibility of supervising the kitchen staff. He entered service on September 22, 1944, and received his discharge on November 25, 1946. (Courtesy of Marleen Gold.)

PFC Percy S. Lynn, Battery B, 483rd AAA AW Battalion, was an anti-aircraft machine gunner on a .50-caliber weapon for 29 months. His unit was one of the very few U.S. Army units that participated in the invasion of Iwo Jima. (Courtesy of Percy S. Lynn and Ned Cash.)

Members of the 2nd Platoon, Section 8, B Battery, 483rd AAA AW Battalion, from left to right, are (front row) James "Pop" Jones, unidentified, George Stathis; (second row) Raymond Young, John Ashton, Stanley Luba, John Simpson, Percy Lynn, Martin Foertsch, unidentified, and John Hayes. Not pictured are Maxie Cooper and Alexander Koproski. Percy recalled that his unit had three .50-caliber machine guns, three range finders, one quad .50-caliber mounted on a trailer, and one 40-mm mounted on a frame pulled by a truck. (Courtesy of Percy S. Lynn and Ned Cash.)

Pictured above is a U.S. Marine Corps tank advancing across the battered black sands against the entrenched Japanese. (Courtesy of Percy S. Lynn and Ned Cash.)

James Henry Padgett, U.S. Army, was among the army troops participating in the invasion of Okinawa. When his knee locked and became immobile, he had to be transported out of the foxhole, placed on a stretcher, and sent away for medical aid. On Okinawa, the G.I.s and the U.S. Marines faced a Japanese enemy who had honeycombed the southern part of the island with concrete bunkers, pillboxes, spider holes, and lateral trenches. The ensuing battle was horrific almost beyond words. (Courtesy of Lorene P. Hopson.)

Yates Padgett, brother of James Henry Padgett and Lorene Padgett Hopson served in the China-Burma-India Theater, probably the most ignored of any location where American forces served in World War II. These troops, 12,000 miles from home, found themselves at the far end of the supply chain and battling the determined enemy and the hostile climate. (Courtesy of Lorene P. Hopson.)

Ten

SERVING ON THE HOME FRONT (1941–1945)

DOING OUR PART

Over 16 million men and women served in the armed forces during World War II. Countless others labored on the home front. Their home-front duties included working in defense industries, maintaining farms and households, raising money for "E" bonds, operating factories, providing entertainment for the soldiers, praying for the safe return of loved ones, and keeping the home fires burning. Important activities to elevate the morale of our troops included packing tidbits for those away from home and keeping up a steady flow of correspondence.

Lavonia Cole Wilkie Radford was working at Stonecutter Mill while living on the family farm. Her husband, Judd Wilkie (page 30) was in the service. This photo of Judd and Lavonia shows the two together while he was home on leave. She recalls how her parents sold peaches to supplement the family income. (Courtesy of Lavonia Cole Wilkie Radford.)

Nettie Owensby Price, like many other Cleveland County mothers, gave some of her dearest possessions to the war effort: her children. She had three sons in service: Falls W. Price, Roy Donald Price, and Arthur F. Price. Mothers who lost a child in service displayed a gold star pin, like the one at the top of the photograph. Mrs. P.R. Price was a gold-star mother because one of her sons, Arthur F. Price (page 57) died on December 28, 1944. (Courtesy of Carolyn Grindstaff Barbee and the co-author.)

With World War II over, Thomas E. Wright of Shelby was able to resume his professional baseball career with the Boston Red Sox. The 5-foot 11-inch, 185-pound outfielder played in 341 games between 1948 and 1956 with the Red Sox, Chicago White Sox, St. Louis Browns, and Washington Senators. He compiled a career batting average of .255. Wright was an above-average defensive outfielder. (Courtesy of Thomas E. Wright.)

T4g. Hoyt B. Howington, 7852nd Quartermaster Service Company, served as a butcher in the Occupation of Germany. He served two years, nine months, and eight days overseas and received the World War II Victory Medal and the Army of Occupation Medal (Germany). His brothers included Hugh Q. Howington, Hal W. Howington (U.S. Army), Nolan P. Howington, and William C. Howington. (Courtesy of Hal W. Howington.)

Janette Walker Williams is pictured with her husband, Capt. Hugh Otto "Toby" Williams, in Texas. The two married in 1943. Like many women, she preserved copies of her husband's letters home. (Courtesy of Jan Williams, daughter.)

Sgt. James Edwin Spangler, 348th Army Air Force Base Unit, served as an aircraft mechanic on B-17s, B-20s, and B-24s. Spangler received the American Theater Campaign Medal and the Good Conduct Medal. (Courtesy of James Edwin Spangler.)

Evan M. Wilson was a civilian flight instructor of the United States Army Air Forces in Bennettsville, South Carolina, for one year between 1944 and 1945. Wilson took a year of leave from his teaching position at Piedmont High School in Lawndale, North Carolina. His wife was Nell Harris Wilson, and his daughters were Lavada Wilson Sain of South Daytona Beach, Florida, and Bertha Wilson Stone of Cherryville, North Carolina. (Courtesy of Lavada Wilson Sain.)

Cpl. Junius Lee Mitcham was an aircraft mechanic on P-38s in California. He was stationed at 43 Base Headquarters and Air Base Squadron AAF. After the war, he was a plant supervisor at the Mauney Cotton Mill. He was married to Lillie Mae Guyton, and his parents were Luther Ransom and Rachel L. Herndon Mitcham. His four daughters include Ethel Irene Hayes, Cubie Lee Dunn, Margaret Frances Williams, and Mildred Elizabeth Bowman. (Courtesy of granddaughter Rachel Haynes Tanner.)

Montrose Pallen Meacham was the daughter of Lt. Earl (page 71) and Montrose McBrayer Mull Meacham. It seemed perfectly natural to 18-month-old Montrose Pallen to dress in uniform like her father. When she appeared on the streets of Shelby, men and women in the armed forces regularly saluted her. She would immediately return the salute with poise and skill. (Courtesy of Lacy Meacham Ballard.)

Sgt. Robert F. Price served in the 2530th US Army Air Force Base Unit as a radio mechanic. He served at Miami Beach; Madison, Wisconsin; Chanute Field, Illinois; and Boca Raton, Florida. He was a motion picture projectionist who showed training films and maintained the film equipment. He received the American Theater Campaign Medal, the World War II Victory Medal, and the Good Conduct Medal. He is the brother of Roy L. Price. (Courtesy of Robert F. Price.)

On May 16, 1943, the USS *MacKenzie* and the USS *Laub* detected and attacked with depth charges an unidentified submarine. Postwar records identify the vessel as the German U-182, lost with no survivors. The *MacKenzie* participated in the invasions of Sicily, Anzio, and Southern France. The *MacKenzie* earned four Battle Stars and the EAME Campaign Medal. S1c. Roy L. Price served aboard the USS *MacKenzie* in the European Theater of Operations. He is the brother of Robert F. Price. (Courtesy of the Cummins and Price families.)

PFC Carmel Matthew Wellmon received his training at Shepard Field, Texas, and Rosecrans Field, Missouri. He served in the Army Transportation Corps and in the Overseas Replacement Depot in Greensboro, North Carolina. He grew up on a cotton farm in Cleveland County. After service he entered college on the Montgomery G.I. Bill and graduated from college in 1950. He taught for 32 years in North Carolina. "God gave my wife Ruth and me two daughters." (Courtesy of Carmel Wellmon.)

PFC Tracy M. Stewart Sr. was in the Medical Detachment, SCU 1908, Camp Cooke, California. He served as a chauffeur and received the Good Conduct Medal. He entered service on March 18, 1942. (Courtesy of Tracy M. Stewart Jr.)

T5g. Glenn H. Geer, Company A, 3908th Signal Service Battalion, was inducted into service on September 2, 1942. He served at Camp Livingston, Louisiana, and the 58th General Hospital. His duties included that of a stock clerk. He received his discharge on October 26, 1945. He earned the EAME Campaign Medal and the Good Conduct Medal. (Courtesy of the family of Glenn H. Geer.)

PFC Johnie F. Greene Jr., Battery G, 22nd Coastal Artillery Battalion received training as a searchlight crewman. He saw service at Portsmouth, New Hampshire; Philadelphia, Pennsylvania; and Fort Bragg, North Carolina. His unit laid sea mines; some were free-floating mines, and some were submerged. He also worked with radar. He received the American Theater Campaign Medal, the World War II Victory Medal, and the Good Conduct Medal. He qualified as a marksman with a .30-caliber rifle. (Courtesy of Johnie F. Greene.)

During World War II, Edward Rollins Price performed a duty as a civilian that was vital. He served as a fireman and later an engineer on Seaboard Air Line Railway trains that ran between Monroe and Rutherfordton, North Carolina. Many of the passengers were service personnel. Edward, in his railroad cap, stands in front of Grindstaff's Store on Highway 74 in Ellenboro, North Carolina. After the war, Ed owned and operated for a while an antique store and grocery store in Cleveland County. (Courtesy of Jeanne Price.)

Pictured here at the Cleveland County Fair are Fred Casey and Aleth McCurry (Casey). This first date resulted into an eventual marriage. James Fred Casey Jr. served in the U.S. Army Corps of Engineers. Casey was drafted in 1942. He was released from duty after the birth of their child Elaine. Casey received a second draft notice in 1944 and entered service again. It was indeed an unusual occurrence to be drafted twice. (Courtesy of Mrs. James Fred Casey Jr.)

T3g. Helen Williams (Bullock) served at the Vint Hill Farm Field Station in Warrenton, Virginia. Vint Hill was a classified intelligence unit with radio interceptors, cryptographers, and radio repair technicians. She served at Vint Hill from June 1943 until June 1945. Women like Bullock replaced soldiers until there were 160 women in the unit. Her unit twice received commendation. At war's end she received the Good Conduct Medal. This photo shows Helen in Kansas City in 1943. (Courtesy of Helen Williams [Bullock] and Jan Williams.)

Rachel Heavner (Dixon) worked at Draft Board 3 in Cherryville, North Carolina. She was under the supervision of Chairman J.T. Allen. Rachel recalled times when they would send four busloads of boys to service. She went to work at the draft board when she was 18 and worked there until the war ended. This board served Cherryville, Dallas, and Bessemer City. She married Richard Raymon Dixon (page 46). (Courtesy of Rachel Heavner Dixon.)

Alice Inez Swofford (Cummins) attended Hollis High School and went to work for the FBI in Washington, D.C., in 1945. Pictured with her are Velma Gregerson (left) and Jean Bates (right). Alice Inez (center) met her future husband Ernest Cummins (page 38) in Washington after the war, and they married on June 27, 1946. She and her husband now reside in Cleveland County, North Carolina. (Courtesy of Alice Inez Swofford Cummins.)

T4g. William Morgan received assignment to the Oak Ridge Facilities in Oak Ridge, Tennessee. Also stationed at this facility was Lorene Padgett Hopson. Their duties were classified. (Courtesy of Lorene Padgett Hopson.)

From January 1938 until 1940, Falls W. Price served in Battery C, First Coastal Artillery Battalion, in the Panama Canal Zone. Falls was a breechman of a 14-inch gun; his task was closing the breech on the gun. These mighty weapons protected the Caribbean Sea entrance to the Panama Canal. As a champion welter-weight boxer, he represented his unit well. He attributes his quick hands to the cotton fields, where he could pick 400 to 500 pounds easily in only one day. (Courtesy of Falls W. Price.)

Hugh Martin Rollins served in the South Pacific and in the postwar German occupation. While he was in the South Pacific, he apparently contracted malaria. This photograph shows him shortly after his release from the military hospital. His brother Spurgeon Brenton Rollins also served. (Courtesy of Mrs. Laddie Brackett.)

T.Sgt. Spurgeon Brenton Rollins participated in the Normandy Invasion and the occupation of Germany. He and his brother, Hugh Martin Rollins, were the sons of Rush Rollins and Verdie Hunt Rollins. (Courtesy of Mrs. Laddie Brackett.)

Martha McCrary (Price) was a member of WAVES (Women Accepted for Volunteer Emergency Service) stationed at a naval facility near Elizabeth City, North Carolina. After the war, she and her husband lived at the Cleveland–Rutherford County line. Her husband, Falls W. Price, owned and operated a store at the line and in Casar; he also managed a farm. Falls remembers that Martha was one of the best dancers anyone had seen. When they danced together, other dancers would stop and watch. (Courtesy of Mary Ruth Price and Falls W. Price.)

An unforgettable basic training exercise was that of entering a building with smoke and gas, having to don a gas mask, and clearing it before exiting the structure. Here, PFC Martin C. Wilkie Jr., 12th Air Depot Group, 5th Air Force, models the typical government-issued device. Thankfully poison gas was not common during World War II. (Courtesy of Martin Wilkie.)

Like many other women of the World War II era, Nell Daves Price faced life at home without her husband, Arthur F. Price. With her three-month-old daughter, Nell moved in with her in-laws. After Arthur's basic training, he returned home on furlough before being shipped overseas. The young couple spent one of their evenings together at the Colfax Free Fair. Cpl. Arthur F. Price did not return at the end of the war; he died on December 28, 1944. Nell became a 21-year-old widow. (Courtesy of Anita Price Davis.)

To ensure a variety of reading material even in the most remote places of the world, the Council on Books in Wartime developed a book designed to fit the pocket of the fatigues. These paperback volumes were about 5 inches by 4 inches. Both classics and current books in an unabridged format were available free of charge in an overseas edition. The Special Services Division of the Army and the Bureau of Naval Personnel distributed these books. (Courtesy of Anita Price Davis.)

Uncle Sam was a constant image across the nation. His pointing finger reminded Americans of the need for sacrifice, devotion, and service in the struggle for freedom. (Courtesy of Anita Price Davis and the U.S. Printing Office.)

Ode to an LST

I think that I shall never see
A worse ship than an LST:
A ship with graceful lines resemblin'
A mud scow fashioned by a gremlin;
A ship whose paint disintegrates
From salt and lesser phosphates;
A ship whose steering engine works
With grunts and groans and nervous jerks;
A ship that doesn't run, but trots;
That labors doing seven knots.
Most any ship will try to please
But only God loves LSTs.

An unknown author wrote these lines, which was copied from the LST 794's 1945 Christmas dinner menu. (Courtesy of William Keever Hamrick.)

Index